A Gap in the Spectrum

Other titles by Marilyn Duckworth

A Barbarous Tongue
The Matchbox House
Over the Fence is Out
Disorderly Conduct
Married Alive

A Gap in the Spectrum

MARILYN DUCKWORTH

Auckland
OXFORD UNIVERSITY PRESS
Oxford Melbourne

Oxford University Press

Oxford New York Toronto Melbourne Auckland
Kuala Lumpur Singapore Hong Kong Tokyo
Delhi Bombay Calcutta Madras Karachi
Nairobi Dar es Salaam Cape Town
and associates in
Beirut Berlin Ibadan Nicosia

First published in 1959 by Hutchinson of London
in the series New Authors Limited. Reproduced from
the original setting by arrangement with the publishers,
and reprinted as a New Zealand Classic in 1985.

© Marilyn Duckworth 1959
This edition © Marilyn Duckworth 1985

This book is copyright. Apart from any
fair dealing for the purpose of private study,
research, criticism or review, as permitted under
the Copyright Act, no part may be reproduced by
any process without the prior permission of
the Oxford University Press

ISBN 0 19 558143 1

Cover designed by John McNulty
Printed in Hong Kong
Published by Oxford University Press
5 Ramsgate Street, Auckland 5, New Zealand

I

I REMEMBER the calico sleeping-bag, and how my body was young and tight against it. It must have been a long time ago, and in a different place. The air is quite a different colour here. I don't know when I first began to notice it, but gradually it has crept up on me—the different colour of the air—the different taste of the water. It has a certain saltiness. But no one else has noticed it. I think I must have come from some very sweet place—sweet and lukewarm, and the sky the colour of breath.

The calico sleeping-bag.... I was sleeping there for a special reason. It was exciting. This word 'exciting' flings up in my memory, but the accompanying emotion seems queerly absent. I know I was waiting for some new experience—perhaps to be married. Yes, it was the virgin's calico. How clear it seems to be growing now. I could feel my coiled plaits, bumpy under my neck—what a lot of hair I had. I felt so beautiful. The perfume of the ointment rubbed into my skin, mingled with the masculine smell of the rush mat, and the harsh effect twanged in my nostrils. Perspiration ran down salty into the corners of my mouth. It was one of the warmer weeks, but never so warm as it can be here.

This place is London—or, yes, England. I always get the two mixed up. You see, it was London where I first woke up, that funny, confused morning.

I had been dreaming of the pre-wedding ceremony the day before—the drums, the wooden flutes, and then the lamp dance and the big dark tree lit up in bright blue. I still had flecks of gold-dust, which my aunts had spent so much time combing through my hair, when I woke.

I sat up immediately and felt my eyes contract in amazement. At first I thought I had been ill and they had moved me to some kind of hospital. Then I thought perhaps I had been married already and was suffering from a loss of memory. But the bed hardly seemed like that of a young bride. There was an inkstain on the crumpled sheet, and an old mauve coverlet had half slid off the bed and was trailing on the threadbare carpet. I was surrounded by that sort of remote feeling which you have in dreams—that things are not to be taken quite seriously, that you can always wake up. I have never quite rid myself of that feeling since. However, my mind was functioning very clearly and I put my head back to think again about this problem. I immediately saw a long, faded curtain by my hand and bounced up on my heels to see if there was a window behind it. There was, but my first relief ebbed suddenly when I saw the view.

A smoky-brown wall loomed up immediately opposite. Pressing my face up close to the glass and peering down, I saw a broken skylight in a lower roof and a small courtyard beyond. A yellow fog brooded over the scene, and, having noticed this, I could all at once smell it seeping under the windows. It was so dingy, so unlike the space and freedom I had been used to, that I was certain now I was being held against my will. Instinctively I ran for the door, and was almost jerked off my balance when it opened so easily.

A long corridor, dimly lit, with doors at intervals on either side, was relieved only by a big black sideboard, chequered with white squares, which I took to be letters, laid out in heaps. To my right the corridor turned a corner and ended in a little, dark flight of stairs.

I was about to take a step forward when I noticed a pair of ugly, thick socks on my feet, and my eyes travelled up to baggy, pink pyjamas. Swinging the door back I discovered a rather pretty blue housecoat on the hook, so slipped my arms into it and padded warily down the corridor.

I had been right about the white squares on the sideboard. They were letters. Turning them over hurriedly in my hand I noted that they were addressed to Cadogan Square, London, England. These last two names seemed oddly familiar. While I tried to place them, my eyes swept along the corridor to the banister of a broad stairway, carpeted far more sumptuously than the rest of the corridor. It seemed a very big house. This was borne out by the number of various names on the letters. I noticed amongst them a duchess and a Lady Blanchard.

Then, suddenly, my eyes leapt back from a blue airmail form, almost in fright. It bore my own name—*Diana Clouston*. I turned it over, focussing impatiently on the sender's name and address. Here I drew a blank. *Robert Stretley, Mata Rd., Wellington, New Zealand.*

'Never heard of him,' I mumbled. A jangle of metal sounded behind me and I jerked round to see a little woman in a tight black frock, with a bunch of keys dangling at her waist. She smiled rather foolishly, and immediately her battered face reminded me of an old breadboard we had had since I was a child.

'Looking for your mail, dear?'

'Yes,' I gasped quickly, and waited, not knowing if I should say anything more.

'I didn't hear you come down to get any supper last night,' the woman went on. 'Did you run out of pennies for the gas? I've told you to ask me if you do. We're always up late listening to the wireless.'

'Thank you. I wasn't hungry last night.'

The woman shook her head disapprovingly and moved off down the corridor. I watched her out of sight, hypnotized by the keys bouncing on her hip, then ran back to my room clutching the air-letter in my pocket.

My first impulse was to tear the letter open immediately, but suddenly a peculiar feeling came upon me. Halfway to the flap my finger stopped and trembled and I froze in this position for some seconds, unable to move. Thoughts came flooding into my mind. Who was I? What had I been up till now, in this funny, new place? Did I even look the same? Turning slowly I jumped to see someone staring at me out of the mirror. It was my old, familiar face—smooth, mousy hair and small, pointed chin. Hot with relief I tore at the letter, spread it on the bed and began to read.

Darling, Darling,

I love you. [I started, laughed, then went on reading.] *Nothing much has been happening lately of interest. I went up to Ardmore with the boys, but it was pretty punk compared to last year. I went on the back of Steve's bike which is going like a bomb now. Brian deserted Sue at the last minute and came with us. Barry was there, or did I tell you? Does he write to you, because I'm not jealous any more. I know you love me. When are you going to get a job? I suppose you're doing a lot of sightseeing in London, but I hope you're not lonely, oceans away from home. . . .*

I stopped reading. I had remembered immediately why the name 'London' seemed familiar, and the memory had chilled me fearfully. It was the name of an imaginary place my sister and I had invented in our childhood and had continued to elaborate on until our early teens. I searched hurriedly for details. We had made it a distorted reflection of the world as we knew it—at the same stage of civilization and made up of entirely the same ingredients. Only the quantities of these ingredients varied. But when I tried to think in what way they had varied, I felt my image of the land receding out of my memory.

With a sensation of rising panic I tried furiously to concentrate. I remembered only one thing more. There had been one new factor, which was the root of the difference between the two worlds. What this new factor was I couldn't decide. All my memories of the imaginary land seemed strangely weak. Thinking about it gave me a feeling of strain and tautness, like when a right-handed person tries to write with his left hand. I gave up trying to concentrate.

All at once the situation struck me with a new force. Was it too fantastic that I had slipped into a complete new world inside my mind? Inside my mind—surely that would mean I had lost control of my mind—was insane? My head began to buzz and I felt my sight fading on the little room and turning inwards towards my confused memory. It was all so absurd. It couldn't be anything but a dream. I gave myself a shake, sighed and picked up the letter again. My head cleared as I read. From it I gleaned several things.

Firstly I was attached, possibly engaged to someone in New Zealand. Robert mentioned a flat in Wellington, and Ngaire, presumably my flat-mate. There was no mention of my parents and I wondered if they were dead. I felt relief more than anything, at this.

Really, the writing was horrible. I smiled to myself as I glanced at the crooked lines. It was odd how I could summon up no feeling towards this Robert who 'knew I loved him'. He struck no chord whatever in my mind. Perhaps if I saw a photograph . . . I moved instinctively towards a squat, varnished desk in the corner of the room, but my attention was arrested by a fat kitchen clock, whose loud ticking seemed suddenly purposeful. Eleven o'clock. I was hungry.

The woman in black had mentioned a kitchen—pennies for the gas. I opened the door of a large cupboard in search of food. It was cluttered with underclothes, a hat, a plate, knife and fork, a small saucepan and a blue plastic beaker. I moved the saucepan aside and came upon some butter labelled 'margarine', a packet of rye biscuits, a tin of coffee and a bag of sugar. This was all. The untidiness surprised me almost as much as anything else. I had always kept my belongings in such order. Or at least, I thought I had. Puzzling over this I began to fold the underclothes neatly and looked around for somewhere else to stow them.

The wardrobe disclosed even clumsier disarray, so I gave up all at once and dumped them back on the floor of the food cupboard. At least I would make the bed. Patting the mauve coverlet into place I caught sight of a small black handbag lying open on the floor. It contained, among lipsticks and dirty handkerchiefs, a purse of small change.

Within a quarter of an hour I came out into the corridor again, wearing a grey skirt, green jumper and an enveloping pink coat. There was nobody in sight. Feeling oddly criminal, I walked quietly past the black sideboard and turned the corner to meet a big brown door. It was open, and I felt a sudden urge to run.

Outside I gasped and stared. It had been snowing, although at the time I didn't recognize the phenomenon. I had never been so cold! As I said before I have also been hot in London —hotter than I had ever known in my old land—Micald. Turning the corner of Pont Street I walked quickly towards Sloane Square. I felt my feet swing in an irregular, jerky way, as if I was on the stage and not quite sure of the stage directions. Every time my dusty suède shoes fell on the hard snow, the cold slapped the underneaths of my feet and propelled me forward. Nervously I was noting the name of the street I was in and of the square I was approaching.

A narrow red bus swished past me and came to a stop. At that exact moment I was conscious of a sharp pain in my eyes, which made me duck my head into my hands. The pain eased at once, and I glanced quickly at the place names on the back of the bus before pulling myself up on to the platform.

'Chelsea,' I told the conductor doubtfully.

'You're going in the wrong direction, miss.' He smirked at another passenger.

'Oh, it doesn't matter.'

'Where do you want then? Piccadilly?'

'Yes, please.'

He shrugged, giving me twopence change with my ticket. Suddenly I felt quite happy. I flopped down and wriggled my stiff feet. Piccadilly, Piccadilly—a funny toy name. I couldn't help feeling happy. I watched the bus route with an excited curiosity, forgetting to note the names of the streets, but staring at the shop windows, the wideness of the streets and the big gates of Hyde Park.

'Piccadilly Circus!'

I jumped down and stared about me. I've seen Piccadilly several times since then, and now it seems funny to say that it made no impression on me at all. It was a place. It was the place where I was going to get something to eat—that was all.

I noticed a restaurant over the road, but when I crossed and looked at the menu outside I found it was too expensive for me. Farther along I came to a coffee-bar with old-fashioned green windows and a contemporary interior.

'Cappucino?' I was asked briskly.

'Yes, one, please,' I agreed, not quite sure what this was. Immediately a thought struck me—What a good thing that in this other world the language common in our country was used. 'And a piece of mince tart,' I indicated, with a nervous croak in my voice.

The waiter edged a slab on to a plate and slapped down a second knife. I tried to look nonchalant, while wondering how these people managed to eat with two knives. Suddenly he gave a cry of laughter and snatched up one knife to replace it with a fork. He mumbled something to his mate and they both turned to me with a look of amusement. Embarrassed, I stumbled quickly to a corner, spilling a froth of coffee in the saucer.

Out of my window opposite I could see two soldiers having a shoe-shine. Looking at the scene I was once again conscious of the pain in my head, so sharp that for a moment I thought

I was going to retch. A second later it had passed. Soldiers were a common enough sight in Micald, for our young men trained regularly, though there hadn't been a war in my lifetime. But it was at the shoe-shiner I found myself staring in a hypnotic manner. At the colour of his coat—a shiny, glowing, crackling colour. Red.

My eyes ached as I stared, and as I continued staring the ache began to fade a little. I was left instead with an impression of rawness, nakedness and exciting defencelessness. It reminded me of how one's finger feels after the days'-old sticky plaster has been removed from it. I took a deep breath and listened to it shake all the way down. I felt completely different—new, excited and expectant.

The mince pie was very good. I crammed the last bite impatiently into my mouth and raised my eyes again stubbornly to the red-coated shoe-shiner. The pain returned, but I went on staring until it seemed to dim and fade to a dull discomfort. Feeling I had achieved something I tucked my black handbag under my arm, where it already felt at home, and walked confidently out into the cold street.

I don't know how long I paraded around the West End in this exalted mood, staring at the challenging, red advertisements, the red lips and scarves and shoes milling past me. But I suddenly noticed I was very tired and stumbled into the nearest Tube station which had fascinated me earlier. Here I studied the map in a nightmare fashion, until a friendly woman established the fact that I wouldn't need to change for Knightsbridge.

'But I want Sloane Street,' I protested.

'That's right,' she nodded.

So I stepped trustfully into the carriage. By good luck

rather than anything else I found my way home. I call it home now, and at the time, in the light of my weariness, I welcomed it as such. The big door was shut and I fished instinctively in my deep pocket for a key. I found one, but was too sleepy to register any relief when it fitted the lock. The warm air in the hall caressed my windburnt face and my eyes felt cold in their sockets.

This is all I remember of that first day. Although it wasn't yet evening, I almost fell out of my coat and on to the soft and lumpy bed.

I woke again before the morning. The light was still on and I got up clumsily to turn it off. As my hand lifted to the switch a flash of fear woke me completely. I turned round slowly, realizing the silence and loneliness of the little room. Clearing my throat loudly, I sat down on the one chair and ran my fingers up and down the arm in five-finger exercises. I was certainly afraid to go back to bed. As I leant back there was a crackle, and I pulled out a crushed packet of cigarettes from behind me. They smelt rather strong, but for the sake of something to do I lit one and went to the mirror, where I drew nonchalant breaths and puffed grey whorls of smoke into my sleepy reflection.

A series of moods began to parade through my mind—childish elation, a sophisticated cynicism, followed by a feeling of abandoned recklessness. I pulled the appropriate faces, talking conversationally to my reflection, drawing my hair up into a pony-tail, a bun. But at the end my face crumpled. I felt sick. Water kept rising into my mouth and to swallow the warm liquid made me shudder—even my elbows.

I slid down on to the bed again, and curled my knees up.

It was so cold. But the pressure of my knees on my stomach made me feel even worse, so I stretched out and tensed myself for the cold to hit me. My fingers fell on a big, crumpled handkerchief, and as if the idea had only just been suggested to me I began to cry feebly, groaning and dribbling the warm saliva out of one side of my mouth. I had never been sick on my own before, that I could remember. Where on earth did I belong? An angry indignation rose suddenly in me. I must belong to someone. Why didn't they come and get me? Had I always lived here? Where were my friends? And I hadn't any money!

I had the feeling that if I was sorry enough for myself something would happen to alter the situation. I had a quaint faith in fate. Fate wouldn't let me be alone and miserable if she only knew about it. Fate would have to be told. So I went on informing her for the next half-hour, into a miserably wet pillow. Then fell asleep.

2

THE clock had stopped and I had lost all idea of the time. Lying lazily on the bed, I looked at my crumpled skirt and jumper, the array of objects on the desk-top, the trail of powder on the carpet. Gradually a feeling of disgust crawled into my mind and suddenly I sat up. For heaven's sake, the place was in a mess! And I'd always had such a reputation for tidiness! Of course, I wasn't me now—or at least . . . I refused to think about it, but instead began to wonder where I could have a bath.

The house was silent, as it had been yesterday, and when I opened my door there was no one in sight. I had not yet explored the narrow corridor to my right, and doing so I found what I had been looking for. The bathroom was cold and smutty, but there was a trickle of warm water in the hot tap. I washed thoroughly and began to feel better.

Back in my room I surveyed the coat-hangers in my wardrobe doubtfully. There was not much choice—another skirt, two jumpers and a taffeta frock. I changed my skirt and began to put up my hair in a pony-tail. But it looked rather silly, so I tied the ribbon flat on the nape of my neck, as I usually did. Then I started methodically to tidy the room. It was a slow job, because I kept coming across new clues to my identity in this world.

My first find was a photograph album. I opened it with a curious feeling of trespassing. Well, there I was, accompanied by strangers, at dances, in the street, on the beach. The photos didn't seem in character with myself at all. They gave the impression that I spent most of my time enjoying myself, and I felt a strange pang of envy that I could remember none of this. Most of the snapshots had names and dates alongside, and I stared intently at the recurring face of 'Robert'. He was pale, with straight, dark hair and a wide grin which gave him a faintly elfish look. He seemed interesting, but struck no responsive note in me.

I went on tidying reluctantly, until I was happily sidetracked by a big, brown envelope bulging with air-letters from New Zealand. They were mostly from Robert, written in a minute scrawl that was painful to decipher. I persevered for some time, until I had reached the conclusion that he talked mostly about himself, with 'I love you's' interspersed at tactful intervals. They contained few clues about myself, so I dived deeper into the envelope.

There were several letters from a Barry Morrison, who seemed on surprisingly intimate terms with me, and poured out the pornographic details of his love affairs without inhibitions. I was at once shocked and amused, and wondered what our relationship could possibly have been. Then I remembered Robert had mentioned a 'Barry' in his last letter. Yes, there it was—*Does Barry write to you, because I'm not jealous any more*. Then there had been something between us, though there was no mention of it in Barry's letters.

The remaining few letters were from 'Mummy', and I

noted this fact with mixed feelings. She could hardly be the mother I had left behind me in my old land. Besides, I had never called her 'Mummy'. And surely she would notice the change in me—my lack of reaction in certain things? The feeling of panic began to flood back again and I quickly tried to reason with myself. After all, Robert had described London as 'oceans way' from New Zealand, so I probably wouldn't be seeing her for some time.

I opened the letter more calmly, but soon discovered that she was writing not from New Zealand but from a place called America, where she seemed to be holidaying with my father. She mentioned coming to England, but didn't state when. *I've picked up some nice things for your trousseau over here, but we'll have to go shopping together in London for your wedding dress*, she went on.

I didn't know what 'trousseau' meant—we had no word for it—but the mention of a wedding dress confirmed my suspicions that I was engaged to Robert. This didn't worry me unduly. I would break it off after a feasible length of time. I reflected suddenly that I would not have come to this decision so casually had I been back in Micald, surrounded by my family. Perhaps I was losing my sense of responsibility? With this thought I closed the envelope briskly and stacked it away in the desk. At least I would retain my tidy habits.

By this time I had a pile of old newspapers, paper-bags and other rubbish accumulated in the middle of the floor. There was no wastepaper-basket, although stuffed down the side of the desk were two big carrier-bags, labelled 'Marks and Spencer', overflowing with damp-smelling waste paper. I considered for a moment how to dispose of this and the other rubbish. Then I remembered that I had noticed a rubbish bin in the little courtyard out of my window. It was a question of finding my way down there.

With a carrier-bag squashed under each arm, I passed the bathroom on my way to the little, dark stairs. They descended in a dusty spiral and I found myself in a passageway opposite the open door of what appeared to be a kitchen. It was bare except for a scrubbed wooden table, a grubby gas-stove, a kettle and a box of matches. I could hear a radio going in the next room. There was a broken skylight at the end of the kitchen, and, remembering this landmark from the view out of my window, I moved across to the outside door and found myself in the courtyard.

I was coming back into the kitchen when I heard voices. The woman in black, who I had decided was the housekeeper, came in. She was followed by a very tall, extremely thin girl in a blue housecoat, who was saying:

'Be an angel, Mrs Reid, and get me something to eat. Just toast and butter or anything. I haven't had a bite since breakfast yesterday—couldn't get out of bed.'

She certainly looked ill, with dark smears under her eyes, and since she was the first fellow inhabitant I had seen, I stared at her with interest. Neither of them had appeared to notice me and I suddenly had the odd sensation that they couldn't see me. So rather loudly I said: 'Hallo!'

Mrs Reid jumped and I with her, then she added:

'Hallo, dear, getting your cup of coffee?'

'Well, yes,' I sighed with relief. 'I suppose I could,' and ran upstairs for the coffee-tin and blue beaker.

While I drank my coffee I listened to a little radio which I had discovered on the floor by the cupboard. I was waiting to find out the time. The programmes seemed disappointingly like the ones I had been used to, except for a slight difference of accent. At any moment I expected them to announce: 'This is Zee line 66,' but instead the voice suddenly informed me: 'This is the BBC Light Programme and the time is ten o'clock.'

I was pleased to find that I must have woken at quite a reasonable hour. I had been beginning to think that the change in atmosphere had upset my metabolism so that I spent more than half my time sleeping. I set the clock, at the same time resolving not to go to bed till ten—my usual bed-time. Having arranged my day in this much of a pattern I sat back on my heels and gave a sigh, almost of contentment.

I noticed how hungry I was. Famished. Just supposing I went down to Mrs Reid and said casually: 'Be an angel and get me something to eat?' I gave a small snort of laughter, then was serious again thinking about the problem of money. Suddenly a thought struck me. Perhaps I had a job and was expected there at this very moment. Perhaps it was pay day. My eyes fluttered swiftly round searching for a clue. Robert had asked: *When are you going to get a job?*, but I could possibly have acquired one since I last wrote to him. How in the world could I find out? Maybe my pockets would hold a clue —a bus ticket, a wage receipt?

I opened the wardrobe door and began to hunt, not very hopefully. Almost at once I came across a rolled-up beret, and out of it fell a wad of notes in a rubber band. Relief leaped up in me as I stooped to count them. Nine in all— enough to last me till I had a job. If I had one already I could now ignore it, but I was beginning to dismiss the idea as improbable. A wave of faintness came over me and I remembered how hungry I was.

I didn't bother to board a bus, but found a Lyons cafeteria in Sloane Square. With two bread rolls and a bar of chocolate I made my way to a table. It wasn't quite so cold as it had been, but the pavements were still snow-covered and for a few minutes I couldn't take my mind off the numbness of my feet. Gradually I began to catch a little of the warmth of the people around me.

All the time I was noticing the recurrence of this colour—red. There seemed to be such a lot of it. It appeared to reflect in people's faces and give them a sort of positive glow.

I had bought a paper on my way in and now looked at it. At home I had never bothered much about reading the news, glancing only briefly at the theatre column and woman's page, so was singularly ignorant in world affairs. For the first time I thought of this as an advantage. Now I could begin afresh without having my brain cluttered with incorrect data. This paper looked, at first glance, much the same as our ones at home, except for the blacker and more startling headlines.

As I read on I felt a disbelieving horror growing on me. Sex crimes, murder, divorce. I couldn't believe that so much had been happening all at about the same time! The thought that tomorrow's newspaper would be as bad made me go cold. I glanced around timidly, trying to imagine these people involved in such crimes. They were eating placidly and reading their newspapers with calm, indifferent interest. I looked back at my folded page. I couldn't understand what could provoke people to do such things, unless they were all a little mad. I wished I was back at home.

I had finished eating, but was reluctant now to leave the warmth of the shop, so remained huddled in my chair, studying the 'Situations Vacant' with little enthusiasm. Things had become unreal again and I was thinking hopefully that I would wake up at any minute. The place was filling up and a woman approached my table doubtfully with a laden tray. I got up and left.

A bus was passing as I looked up and the red glow suddenly revived me. I leapt on to the platform without thinking and held out my fare.

'Piccadilly, please.'

He took it. I was going in the right direction. I was walking along Leicester Square when a picture title caught my eye: *Animal Farm*. I went closer to look at the stills. They were of funny little animals with strong, ferocious expressions, and I began to be interested. As I looked across to the commissionaire, he announced:

'Five shillings only.'

I glanced at the price list and asked him: 'Won't there be any three-and-sixes?'

'Couldn't say, miss. Well, at the start of the new programme there should be,' he added and pointed: 'Queue over there.'

I walked over to where there was the beginning of a queue on the pavement, and pulled my coat around me. Casual conversations drifted to me and I made an effort not to show the morbid interest I felt in them. The peculiar, nagging envy I had felt before on studying the photograph album became strong again.

The people directly behind me seemed to be students—three young men and a girl in an old fur coat. Their conversation was animated and humorous and I felt insipid and half asleep beside them. I could almost see my yellowish-grey face turned flatly upon them. How odd they would think me—if they only noticed me. I stared down at my damp, suède shoes, but a certain fascination made me look up again. The girl was laughing, running her fingers through her thin, dark hair, revealing two excited eyes under her fringe, while the young men leaned forward and talked eagerly.

'I don't like Rubens' women, they all have fat tummies,' the girl was saying petulantly. 'Now, don't fib, Teddy, you hate them too.'

Teddy launched into a long speech, swaying backwards on his heels and accompanying it with extravagant gestures. Soon they all laughed delightedly again. I caught the girl's eye and looked away hurriedly, feeling like some frumpish old maid. I concentrated instead on a serious-faced schoolboy ahead of me who was busy polishing his thick glasses.

'Six three-and-sixes,' the commissionaire rapped out. We hurried forward. Inside the small, hot theatre I found myself placed in the front row with the students filling the seats to one side of me. The film absorbed me. The story progressed tragically to the death of the old horse, and I moved restlessly in my seat, unwilling to submit to the pathos of the scene.

At once I was amazed to notice that the girl beside me was crying fiercely, huddled into her old fur coat. Even one of the young men had slithered as far down in his seat as possible, to hide the wet patches on his cheeks. I went quite cold, as if I had suddenly noticed a danger lurking, and forgot to swallow for a few seconds.

Then a swift shame came over me. All these people were moved—and I—could I be lacking in something? It was an idea I was often to wonder about as time went on, though in my old country it would never have occurred to me. My lack had not stood out against anyone I had known there. In fact I had always been regarded as rather emotional. In this world I had come across something new. I began to be possessed by a longing to share in it. When I had accustomed myself to look at the colour red without being hurt by it, I had achieved part of something but not all.

I picked up the thread of the film and tried to surrender myself to the atmosphere. I even cheated a little and coaxed myself into a half yawn which brought a few tears into my eyes. But the drollness of this struck me suddenly and I could only grin silently down into my lap. The film was continuous and, as I had missed a little of the beginning, I remained seated when it began again. After a short time I heard the students consulting about whether to sit through the whole film a second time. I bargained silently with them. 'Stay, then I will too,' and was relieved when they didn't move.

The film had to end eventually, and emerging from the cinema I found myself alone again. It was dark, so I turned hastily into the nearest Forte's café and perched at the bar with a hamburger. In this comfortable atmosphere of people eating and laughing together I felt relaxed, and the confusion in my brain began to sort itself out.

If this whole thing was a dream I was taking a long time to wake up. Meanwhile I would have to adjust myself to my surroundings. It shouldn't be too difficult, for they differed little outwardly from those I had been used to. There was this new colour, there was the slightly different accent, the more extreme climate. Later I was to find several rather different customs. Thus simplified it made the future look a lot clearer. Of course, there were the more complex problems of how I was to behave when back amongst friends and relatives who presumably knew me well. But at least I would have had time to work things out on my own.

A cautious happiness began to invade me, and I felt a stirring of that adventurous spirit which my mother had attributed to an unconscious wish not to grow up. I thought of 'Mummy' in the letter I had been reading that morning. I wondered about her a little. Then at last I forced myself out into the cold street again.

There was a news-seller by the Piccadilly Tube entrance, his back turned to me in a fawn duffel-coat, though I had no name for it at the time. He turned as I approached to buy a magazine, and I tried to keep the horror out of my face. He had only one eye and his cheek was drawn up into an agonizing twist, leaving his mouth a lipless hole in his torn face. I took my change hurriedly and hurtled down the steps into the Tube station.

At the bottom I stopped and gazed for a moment, unseeingly, at a chocolate slot-machine. I remembered the headlines in the newspaper I had in my pocket. A sense of danger and insecurity had replaced my spirit of adventure. That was a difference between our worlds which I had failed to include in my summing up. This world was full of horrible, meaningless things. I thought how strange it was that people affected so strongly by the death of a horse, in a film, should allow or help such things to occur. Perhaps it was the very fact that their emotions were effected so easily which made them capable of those crimes I had read of. Of course, we had the occasional scandal in my old land—I could even remember a murder in my lifetime—but so much of it was—incredible.

Gradually the slot-machine drew into focus. I pulled myself together sharply and went to buy a ticket. It was crowded in the Tube, and this time the warm roughness of coats rubbing against me didn't seem quite so friendly.

My perceptive powers seemed to have sharpened and all at once I noticed something about the people around me which I had missed before. Some of them were exaggeratedly thin, some terribly fat. Of course, there were the average ones as well, but here and there an extreme stood out, and these seemed to me sinister, even deformed. I didn't take long after this to get used to the fact, but at the time it made me shudder. I remembered a frightening dream I had once had, when things had swelled to abnormal proportions, and then diminished sickeningly.

My sense of insecurity grew. This was a world of extremes. Anything could happen, I thought, not for the first time. Anything, anything.

I almost ran up Sloane Street, with the cold air biting on my face. Past the hotel, the telephone-box, through the wooden doors, oddly churchlike, down the dim hall and into my room. I had left the radio on, and this cheered me a little. Plugging in the small, round heater I noticed my hands were shaking. They were raw with cold, so I warmed them briefly, looking about me for familiar landmarks to calm my nerves. It was late, so I went to bed. I was more tired than I had thought.

Just as I was dropping off to sleep, I woke with a start. My heart was beating wildly and I couldn't quite decide what had happened. It was as if my mind had given a sudden squint and fixed in a twisted position for some seconds before it freed itself.

I was going mad! The idea hit me with force, and for a moment everything reeled. Quite as suddenly everything gained its balance again. Mad. What did the word mean, after all? I would probably be labelled by it, if I tried to tell people of my strange experience of waking up out of another world. If I returned home and told my family of this new world, on the other hand, they too would suspect me of being insane. So what was the difference whether I really was or not? With a brief, hysterical laugh, I turned over and drifted into dreams confused by the radio which continued to play on the chair beside me.

3

NEXT morning the adventurous spirit was back. I could hardly wait to dress and leave my room behind me. I was already accustoming myself to the colder atmosphere, but it occurred to me to wonder if there would be a hot season, as there was at home. It was still quite dark as I walked past Hyde Park towards Piccadilly. In the rather eerie stillness a milkman's horse thudded on the snow, and then there was just the sound of my own suède shoes on the pavement. The sight of the shops, closed and barred, was a lonely one, and I hoped they would soon open and mill with noisy customers. I leaned on a rail at Leicester Square and waited.

After a while I ventured down the steps into the 'Ladies', expecting to find a barred gate. But no, the place was open and inhabited. A fat old woman, naked save for a big pair of bloomers, was sitting placidly on an upturned bucket, mending a petticoat with black thread. Another woman, dressed in a number of cardigans and jumpers, was washing some yellowish garments in the basin. The woman on the bucket took no notice of me as I edged past her expanse of gooseflesh and headed for the second wash-basin. They both went on working calmly, throwing sharp remarks at each other, which I couldn't catch, until I drew my gloves back on and moved towards the stairs.

In the short time I had spent down there it had grown quite light and I had a feeling of things beginning to stir about me. Walking on for some distance I came across an open milk-bar, sending a shaft of light on to the kerb. It was surprisingly full of tired, rather dirty-looking men, having tea and toast. After a moment's hesitation I went in and ordered bacon and eggs.

There was a couple at the table alongside mine, and as I watched the man drew out several yards of bright beads and held them across the table towards his girl friend. For a moment they both gazed at them in delight, before he pocketed them again. I wondered if they had stolen them. In the light of what was reported in the papers, it seemed quite probable. But, then, would they be flourishing them so freely if they had? I laughed at myself for having grown so suspicious in the last few days. I suppose my main problem is a sense of proportion, I reflected. Mine seems quite out of focus according to the values of this place. I should think it will take some time for me to adjust it.

I spent the rest of the day in milk-bars and cafeterias, trying to study the customers unobtrusively and listen to their gossip. Several people had looked at me accusingly, as if they suspected I was spying on them, so at last I gave up and caught the bus back to Cadogan Square.

It was dark when I arrived, though not yet six o'clock. There was a letter for me on the sideboard.

Dear Miss Clouston, it began, and I glanced with surprise towards the signature at the bottom of the page. *Father Spencer*, I puzzled. The rest of the letter puzzled me even more. It seemed I was intending to change my religion! Apparently this required some sort of tuition and I had asked Father Spencer's advice about it. The idea of changing one's religion seemed almost as ludicrous to me as changing one's skin. I had only known one religion in my life—an undemanding set of beliefs which everyone had taken completely for granted. Religion in Micald had played a very unobtrusive part in our lives. For instance, it had nothing to do with the wedding ceremony, and we had no churches. In each large city we had a holy reading-room, where one could read religious works or simply meditate—but these were very little frequented. There were also travelling 'Fathers', who 'brought religion to the homes', but these were often the subject of coarse jokes, and were only taken seriously in the primary schools.

I returned to the letter. Father Spencer had given me the address of a place where lectures were given on the 'Catholic' religion. It was called the 'Grail', and turned out to be in Sloane Street, just around the corner from Cadogan Square. Meetings were every Thursday at eight o'clock.

· · · · ·

I went the following evening. It had been snowing all day, so until then I hadn't ventured outside. Instead I had continued knitting a scarf which I had found half completed, and contented myself with numerous cups of coffee and an occasional biscuit. It was a relief to be out in the air again. When I reached the Grail I found the door open. I walked in hesitantly and began to take my coat off to leave in the hall, as I found others doing. They were talking like old friends and I felt rather foolish, following them up the stairs—as if

I had come to a party uninvited, but that everyone was too polite to mention it.

In the impersonal atmosphere of the lecture-room I began to feel more at home, and relaxed on my hard chair, while a very young priest arranged books on the table and rubbed his hands together contentedly. I was sitting next to two girls of about my own age, who smiled at me in a friendly way. To my surprise, one of them suddenly said:

'Nobody ever talks to you. We've been here three times already, but nobody's ever introduced themselves. They all seem to know each other. I think most of them are Catholics already. Funny, isn't it?'

'I'm Doris and this is Pat,' the other girl intervened.

'I'm Diana.' My voice sounded strained and rusty, and I coughed quickly to cover it.

'Have you been here before?' Pat asked, and went on without waiting for an answer. 'My Dad would be after me with the bread-knife if he knew I came here. He's dead set against Catholics. Oh, you aren't one, are you?'

'No, but my fiancé is,' I replied, then froze in amazement with my lips still parted. I could have sworn I hadn't discovered this from his letters, but the words had fallen so glibly from my tongue, and I was convinced that they were true.

'Ooh, you're not going to turn, are you?' Pat queried. 'Though I think their churches are lovely . . .'

'I suppose your fiancé's been telling you all about it and giving you books and things to read, hasn't he?' asked Doris.

'Yes . . .' I began doubtfully.

'You have to learn the Catechism, don't you?'

'Yes—the Catechism.' The image of a small, red book popped into my mind.

'Why didn't your fiancé bring you here?' Pat prodded.

'He doesn't live here. He lives in New Zealand. I'm just here on holiday.'

'New Zealand? Gosh, isn't she lucky? Oh, he's going to begin,' Doris indicated.

'This one's ever so nice,' Pat whispered. 'We had a lovely argument with him once. But last week there was another one . . .' She stopped at a prod from Doris.

The young priest was saying a short prayer before beginning his talk. He had a smooth, rather thick voice, and stressed his arguments in such a way as to make them seem well thought out and solidly balanced. I began to derive an extraordinary pleasure from sitting there, listening to him, and resolved to read more about what he was saying. I was at a disadvantage not knowing the religious theories he was arguing against. There must be another side of the picture and, though it seemed difficult to imagine while he was talking, I realized that it could probably be argued for, just as logically as the side he was defending. I sighed. It was all very difficult. But now it was time for a break, and a woman with thick legs brought around tea.

'Were you born in New Zealand?' Pat asked as soon as she had helped herself to a cup. 'A girl at work wants to go out there for good, but she can't make up her mind. Do you go to work over here, or is it a real holiday?'

'Well, I haven't a job at the moment, but I'll have to get one soon,' I told her.

'What do you do? Shorthand typing? You can always get a good job with shorthand.'

'No, I—I'm afraid I don't do anything really. I've worked in an office and had a few other odd jobs. You see, I was going to university in New Zealand, and I didn't want a career—just to make a bit of money while I was studying.' I hoped they didn't think it odd that I should talk so slowly, but I had to allow time to feel my way. At the same time I could feel my cheeks beginning to flush with excitement. Here were half my difficulties dissolving! It appeared that when I was in a position that forced me to remember things, my memory made a special effort and worked with miraculous ease.

'What were you going to do after that—university I mean,' Doris broke in.

'I don't know——' lamely.

'Get married, I expect,' Pat grinned. 'That's a full-time job. Funny taste this tea has.'

The priest continued talking for a short time. I made an effort to concentrate again, but this time my mind kept wandering off among my new-found memories. University . . . I remembered now that Robert had mentioned a ''varsity bash' in one of his letters, but at the time it had had only a second-hand force. Now I could visualize a big, red building on a hill, and into my nostrils crept the smell of chalk and cosmetics, the odour of an empty dance hall. I tried to surrender myself into this atmosphere, but suddenly the priest had stopped talking and the chairs creaked loudly around me. Nobody was rising to go, however, merely rearranging themselves, and Doris said:

'We're going to ask him about the Immaculate Conception.'

'Yes, he's sure to get worked up over that,' Pat said with relish. 'Bother those people. I knew they'd bag him first. You're not in a hurry to get home, are you?'

'Oh, no. I live just round the corner in Cadogan Square.'

'Gosh, do you? What is it, a flat?'

'No, just a little room. Very tiny.'

'You live on your own then?'

'Yes.'

'Ooh, I wouldn't like that, would you, Doris?'

'Oh, it's all right really,' I said, with a certain superiority. At the same time I felt a sudden qualm of loneliness.

'Father Rafferty!'

We talked to the priest for about ten minutes. He seemed very pleasant, but I couldn't help noticing how often he used the word 'patently'. It was beginning to jar on me, like a dripping tap, when he was called away by another young priest, wearing a black beret tight down on his forehead.

I followed the two girls out to where we had left our coats, and we walked together down the snowy street, as far as my corner.

'We have to get the Tube,' Doris told me. 'We've got to go all the way to Chislehurst. I expect we'll see you next week though. It's the "Infallibility of the Pope".'

'Yes, you'd better read it up, and we'll have a good go at Father Rafferty. The trouble is he's ready for all the arguments we raise. Oh well.'

They continued on towards Sloane Square. I was smiling to myself as I unlocked the big door.

The next day I went for a walk and found a church.

It was a Catholic church, as I discovered from the board outside, and I approached it with curiosity and expectancy. I was unprepared for the air of gravity and importance I met with inside. This was how I described it mentally at the time, though now I suppose I would place the atmosphere more simply as one of holiness. A round-eyed statue of Mary stared down at me, and my attention was drawn to the other statues, the stained windows, the altar. Several candles were burning in front of one statue—St Anthony—at different lengths. I could see the heads of three women, all wearing scarves, half hidden among the pews, on their knees. Then I noticed an old man muttering in the pew right beside me. He raised his eyes defiantly towards me, without letting up his muttering, and I felt a sudden urge to hurry out of the place.

On the way my eye was caught by a notice in the doorway, about the Grail lectures. I had hardly glanced at it before a deep, cultured voice spoke behind me. I turned to see a man in a dusty, black overcoat and a bowler hat.

'Could you oblige me with a shilling for the price of a bed?' he said for the second time.

'Pardon?' I still hadn't understood, and he had to repeat himself again. I noticed he held his back very straight.

'I'm afraid I can't. I haven't any money with me,' I said truthfully, but still looking puzzled. What a funny thing, I thought, as I moved off. I suppose he wanted it to make up the price of a bed. I had walked some distance before it occurred to me that he needed the money for a night's board. But could there be board anywhere so cheap? I had never come across doss-houses in Micald, but now some inkling that such places existed forced itself upon me. But how terrible, I couldn't help thinking. He had such a nice voice and such a straight back.

When I turned round he had disappeared into the church. Maybe he was going to steal money from the box beside the candles. I intended this thought as a joke, but curiously it made me shudder. Anything could happen in this world, I remembered. Anything at all. I began to run.

4

WHEN I got back there was another letter for me with an English stamp. This one was from 'Aunty Edna'.

Dear Diana [it began],

It was sweet of you to invite us to the ballet, dear. I'm so sorry that I won't be able to come myself, as I have a bad cold, but Josie is coming anyway, and bringing her friend Lesley—you remember her?—as I knew you wouldn't want the tickets to be wasted. I'm sending the tickets back to you, in case Josie's late—you know what she is. So if the programme starts before they come, leave them at the ticket office and they can ask for the tickets for Dunning. I do hope you're feeling better, dear. I suppose it was just a dose of that funny 'flu. Are you doing a lot of sightseeing? I suppose you've visited all your old haunts by now, at Sidcup and Outwood. They'll have changed a lot since you were a little girl, as you found it had here. I'm still keeping the spare room for you, in case you'd like to come back here and get a job later. I hope the ballet is lovely, dear. . . .

I sat looking down at this letter thoughtfully. It seemed to suggest that I had lived in England before, when I was 'a little girl'. I began to wonder how long it had been for—or even if I had been born here, and only spent a few years in

New Zealand. I frowned. There was still so much to learn about myself. Aunty Edna was keeping the spare room for me—apparently I had stayed with them before coming to London. My mind halted around the word 'spare room', and I could feel my memory straining towards it. Yes, there it was, a tiny, cold room with a bookshelf of boys' annuals and a stain of damp on the wallpaper. The clarity of this picture startled me. I was beginning to remember things so well. Supposing I really had lived in this world all my life? Was Micald just a dream, a prolonged delirium? *I do hope you're feeling better, dear*—the words jumped up at me. So I had been ill. But, I reassured myself, it didn't sound serious from the way she talked of it in the letter.

I turned the tickets over in my hand. They were dated for Saturday—tomorrow, I realized with a start. I would be faced by someone who knew me and whom I was supposed to recognize. I was filled with a mixture of excitement and trepidation, and ran trembling fingers up and down the hard edge of the tickets.

Ballet. The word seemed to have a richer sound than I had noticed before. I wondered if it would be the same as our dancing, which was usually held outside. The tickets read 'Covent Garden', which seemed to suggest an outdoor performance, but surely in all this snow . . . ? I shrugged and went to put the tickets in my purse.

I had brought some thick ham sandwiches home with me, instead of eating out. Even so, they had seemed incredibly dear to me—and my coffee-tin was nearly empty. The problem of money began to nag at me, and at last I gave up eating to count how much I had left. I was relieved to find I had more than I'd calculated, but even so, I would have to find a job quite soon. I had told the girls at the Grail that I'd worked in an office—Robert had mentioned this in his letters—but now I began to remember working in a place where food was served, and then in a big place with machines. This would suggest either adaptability or irresponsibility. From what Robert wrote, and from the photograph album, I tended to suspect the latter. Although I was still in possession of my own names, I was convinced by now that the identity I had taken over was very unlike my old one. What I was afraid of was that I would gradually revert to the character my friends and relatives in this world would now expect of me. It would be unwillingly, however. This was all I had left of my real self, and if that were to change or disappear—I—I'd be out of control. I picked up my knitting quickly, to steady myself, and knitted the first two rows without thinking.

The following evening I steamed my suède shoes over the kettle, and dressed to go out with mounting anticipation. For the first time I wondered how old Josie was. How well did I know her? Was she talkative? Would she realize I hadn't recognized her at first sight?

In the Knightsbridge Underground I was about to ask someone how to reach Covent Garden, when the name caught my eye on the wall map. Relieved, I followed the crowd to the escalator. But when I emerged expectantly at the other end, I looked about me in bewilderment. I had hoped to see 'Covent Garden' in big lights, or at least some obvious indication of where it was. After walking up and down, appraising the street, I asked a passer-by to direct me.

'The Opera House?' she queried.

'Oh, yes.' I glanced down at the tickets again.

She directed me and I set off down the dark street she had indicated. It was early yet, for I'd left plenty of time in case I lost myself. I was beginning to think this was what I had done, when suddenly, there it was. An awful wave of disappointment heaved itself at me. The place seemed drab and unimposing—merely another theatre. I took a breath and crossed the road to enter the foyer.

I was nearly an hour early, and was surprised to see such a number of people already there. . . . Many of them were dressed, to my amazement, in long frocks and furs. Most of them looked cold, but their faces glowed in that way so unfamiliar to me. Even children were there in party frocks. I felt very clumsy and stuffy beside all this elegance. I was relieved to see a group of young people in duffel-coats and daytime clothes. Supposing Josie turned up wearing an evening frock? The thought made me go hot.

I glanced quickly at my watch. How could I fill in the time? The idea of waiting around for an hour, not knowing when I was to be pounced upon, wasn't an attractive one. I remembered a small café in the street I had come from, and decided to go there for a warm drink. When the shop door fell to behind me, I found myself in company with a collection of labourers in high-necked pullovers and scarves. They looked at me with faintly derisive smiles, then, to my relief, ignored me. I asked the girl at the counter for a Horlicks, and gratefully warmed my hands on the mug as I steered my way to a distant table.

It was only when I had taken the first sip, that I pulled up with a jerk. It was the very familiarity of the flavour which had taken me by surprise. Now I remembered the ease with which the name had slid off my tongue, although we had had no such drink in Micald. It was almost as if I had two separate memories side by side, both struggling for precedence. The trade names, I realized now, were perhaps the main reason why the shops had looked so strange to me at first, although they were set out in exactly the same way I was used to. However, I felt I would soon accustom myself to them. It appeared, once more, that the less hard I tried to adjust myself to my new surroundings, the easier it became. How well I'm getting things worked out, I thought, taking another warm sip of my drink.

At this moment my eye was caught by a young man sitting opposite, several tables away. He was looking at me with a strangely intimate expression of amusement, and as I stared at him he winked. Immediately I drew myself up and turned away.

This made me think of the man I'd been about to marry in Micald. He had been considerably older than me, and I hadn't known him very well. This may seem strange. But for us, marriage was often just a thing of convenience—I suppose because no one seemed to fall in love in the intense way that happens here. My fiancé had been tall and fair—but now a strange thing happened. I couldn't remember his features! I knew I had found his smile attractive, but now I couldn't visualize it at all. I took a tighter grip on my Horlicks mug, and tried to throw my mind back.

I thought of my mother and my sister. Thank goodness, they were still fresh in my memory. And yet they seemed to be of very little importance to me now. In fact I'd hardly thought of them since waking up in Cadogan Square. I wondered, not for the first time, what was supposed to have happened to me back in Micald. Was I in a coma—dead even? It was a queerly disturbing thought. Supposing one day I woke up to find myself buried alive? I shuddered. It was the sort of thing my sister had been fond of thinking up to frighten me. I suppose it was her idea really, the conception of that imaginary land which we had called England. And yet I had invented far more stories about it. And now here I was! It was unbelievable. By now I had ceased thinking of it as the same place we had conjured up in our minds. I was too deeply involved in it, and it was too real. All the same, it was a disquieting thought that I had lost myself inside something which existed only in my head.

I was beginning to tremble again, when the young man opposite me drew my attention again, by pushing his chair back noisily. I remembered the time and looked anxiously at my watch. Twenty to eight. At least I had passed the time, and now I drew on my gloves, thinking of the meeting with Josie and Lesley.

The foyer was even more crowded when I returned. I took up a position where I could be easily noticed and recognized. I purposely looked preoccupied. Then, when accosted, I would spring to attention as if suddenly roused from a daydream. However, the time went by and nobody spoke to me. I found myself searching the crowd for a likely couple. Slowly the foyer was emptying of people. The programme was about to begin. I remembered then what Aunt Edna had said about leaving the tickets at the desk, so did so. I slipped through the heavy doors just in time.

The curtain was rising as I followed the usher blindly towards my seat. It was on the side, near the front, and I had an excellent view of the stage. I had been so intent on appearing preoccupied, that I had neglected to buy a programme, but at the time it didn't seem to matter.

I was completely enthralled by what I saw before me on the delicately lit stage. It was like nothing I had ever witnessed in the way of dancing before. For one thing, the clothes were much more elaborate, the colours more daring, and the dancers wore shoes. I stared at the prima ballerina as she poised herself effortlessly on her points, and found I was holding my breath.

The only ballet I had known up to now, was that careful stepping and whirling in stockinged feet, on a round, outdoor stage. Usually it was performed in broad daylight, for the days were long. This was accompanied by a small orchestra, and a singer, usually a woman, providing a repetitive kind of narrative. It was some moments before I realized that it was not merely the spectacle that was disturbing me, but also the wild, profound music. I had never heard such emotional music played with such intense feeling. It was nothing like our slow, staid symphonies and jerky minuets in Micald.

The more I listened the more excited I became. It seemed to me that there was something in the music, swelling and straining to burst out of it and fly up to the roof. Then, as I watched, the *corps-de-ballet* suddenly curved, and in that moment of perfection the music seemed to soar and curve in communion with them. I gasped with delight, then quickly dropped my eyes. I found myself weak and trembling. The music went on, but it sounded distant now, for my heart was drumming in my ears. Then I remembered Josie. It amazed me that I had forgotten her, after being so worried about our meeting. The first part of the programme was drawing to a close, however, and I was beginning to think with relief that the two girls weren't coming after all. The curtain fell, and the lights went up.

Feeling relaxed and strangely happy I made my way out and bought a programme. People seemed to be converging up the wide stairs, so I followed them and was delighted to see coffee being served at one end of the bar. I propped myself against the wall with the tiny cup, and tried not to mind my thick, ugly clothes in such surroundings. The next ballet was *Les Patineurs*, according to my programme, which I read hastily, in case the interval should be over too soon.

When I returned downstairs, the two seats beside me were still unoccupied, so with a sigh of contentment I gave myself up to my new-found pleasure.

As I walked towards the Underground afterwards, I was humming snatches of the warm, enchanting music. It was very cold, although it hadn't snowed all day, and the force of it hit me fiercely, contrasting with the warm feeling inside me. I was thankful to reach even the doubtful sanctuary of the draughty lift. I was raising my eyes to study the wall advertisements, when my glance was arrested by a young man, nicely but not flashily dressed. He was leaning a little towards me with an inquiring look, and once his lips parted as if he were going to speak. I half smiled and was going to turn away, when he came towards me, smiling, and said:

'It is you, Diana, isn't it?'

Of course—I hadn't thought that he might know me! I began to stutter. Fortunately he went on:

'I'd only seen you that once, in Redhill, with Josie, since you came over. So I wasn't quite sure. I hope you don't mind.'

'No, that's all right. I was in a bit of a daze myself, as a matter of fact,' I found myself saying.

'Oh? What put you in a daze?'

'I've just been to the ballet. I don't go often, and it quite stunned me. Josie was supposed to come too, but she didn't turn up.' I was delighted to have this much information to offer him, and was surprised at myself for talking so glibly. However, he looked rather blank and I suddenly thought— Suppose he takes me for another Diana? But he was saying:

'That wasn't very nice of her. I don't think she'd be very keen on ballet, anyway. Is she?'

'I suppose not.' I could think of nothing more to say, and followed him in silence along the platform.

'Anyway,' he said, suddenly brightening, 'where are you living in London? Is it far out?' I told him. 'That was lucky,' he looked surprised. 'How did you manage that?'

'A friend found it for me. It's quite cheap.' This fell off my tongue before I'd had time to think about it. In the same moment as wondering if it were true, I wondered when I'd next be expected to pay the rent. The young man was looking at me curiously, but when he met my glance he went on hurriedly.

'Kathleen says to come and visit us one day. She's at art school now, and having a really mad, wonderful time. Maureen could probably help you find a job too. She's got a friend with an agency. Anyway, they're both dying to see you again. Ten years is a long time. They still tell stories of when they belonged to your "Secret Exploring Indians" club.'

He was laughing, and I laughed with him. It was a pleasant sensation. We had boarded the train by now, and he was sheltering me solicitously from a fat, drunk man, whose toes kept appearing to float away from the floor, leaving him rocking on his heels. We watched him together for a moment, then smiled ruefully at each other.

'I get out next stop,' he informed me. 'You couldn't stop off for coffee, could you?'

'Oh, no, I must get home I'm afraid.'

'Well, come up to Redhill, anyhow. We'll work out a job for you. What about a nanny? There's plenty of nanny jobs, I believe.'

'Of what jobs?' I puzzled.

'Nanny. You know, looking after children.' The train had stopped and he was trying to force his way out.

'Well, don't forget,' he waved, smiling. As the train went on I watched him heading for the exit.

5

I WAS wakened next morning by an insistent tapping on my door, and stumbled out of bed to turn the key. Mrs Reid was standing outside, with her hands clasped over her black dress.

'I'm sorry to disturb you, dear, but Lady Blanchard asked me to see you.'

'Yes, what is it?' A sudden apprehension woke me up completely.

'Well, it's about your room. There's a young man wants it. Him what had it before you. And she says there's a nice room upstairs if you wouldn't mind changing.'

'No, that's all right.' I smiled with relief.

'But the other thing is—it's four guineas instead of two.' She looked at me defiantly.

'Oh, I see.' I drew my bed-jacket around me, feeling suddenly at a disadvantage in my night clothes. 'Well——' I really had no idea what to do.

'Look, you think it over, dear. But he's coming Tuesday night, so you'd better not take too long about it. If you do decide to stay, let me know and I'll help you move your things up. The room's empty now, so you can change when you like.'

When she had gone I sat down on the bed and tried to think. I had never seen this Lady Blanchard Mrs Reid spoke of. Apparently she owned the house and, having seen letters for her on the sideboard, I concluded she lived here. But four guineas—twice the amount I had been paying! It seemed a lot to have to pay out regularly. I had a small idea of what wages a girl of my age could earn, from the 'Situations Vacant' column. It would be practically impossible.

I remembered Aunty Edna's offer of the spare bedroom. I had gathered that the Dunnings lived quite close to the young man I had met last night. That would be nice, anyway. I supposed I could write to the address on Aunty Edna's letter. But Josie hadn't turned up. . . . I suddenly couldn't face the idea of almost begging for accommodation. I felt helpless. If I'd only had someone to advise me.

Sighing, I padded out to the sideboard. I felt a swift thrill of pleasure to see two airmail letters waiting for me. They comforted me as would the sight of a good meal.

The first was from Robert, and again his bad writing irritated me. I read it quickly, not bothering to decipher the words which had run into a blur. One sentence struck me: *Are you still knitting a row of your scarf each day, to mark off the time till we're together again?* I thought of the scarf which I had knitted inches of in one afternoon, and a laugh bubbled up inside me. His letter seemed to me terribly sentimental and melodramatic. I wondered what sort of letters I was in the habit of writing to him. He would be bound to notice a difference, when I did write. The idea that I would have to do so soon, worried me slightly, but somehow I couldn't take it seriously.

My mother's letter was also written in a rather hurried, careless style, and tiny, almost illegible postscripts were scrawled around the sides, when she had run out of space. She spent half the letter telling me about the people she had met in America, then went on to say:

Diana, dear, haven't you seen Kathleen Bartlett yet? It's rather rude—being in England all these weeks. You needn't be shy of them. You'll get on well with Kathleen although Maureen's got rather older than her age since Mr Bartlett died. I didn't see Stephen when I was there.

I put the letter down and frowned. Almost certainly, this was the family that the young man of last night belonged to. Stephen—yes! He looked as if he should be called Stephen. I wondered why I hadn't thought of it at the time. I frowned again. It was just what I wanted to do—visit this family—tell them my problem. Stephen had said they would help me find a job. But where did they live? It was unlikely that I would run across Stephen again. I wanted to cry with frustration. All I could do was look for cheap board in the newspaper.

It was while I was looking at the *Daily Mail* that I suddenly remembered seeing an address-book in the desk. If only it would be there. It was. *No. 21 Woodlands Way, Redhill, Surrey.* Giving a contented stretch, I began to dress quickly. I would go immediately and take a chance on their being home. Apprehensive excitement added speed to my movements. It was a familiar sensation by now. Back home I had rarely, if ever, felt very disturbed by anything, presumably because nothing exciting had ever happened to me. For the first time it occurred to me that my life, in fact, all life, in Micald had been very dull. I had no idea of how to get to Redhill or of how far away it was, but at the ticket office at Victoria Station

I was sold a return ticket for only a few shillings and directed to the right platform.

The train seemed extremely dirty to me and I noticed that the girl sitting opposite me had specks of soot in her make-up. She wore mittens and knitted furiously, the tips of her fingers protruding discoloured and defenceless. What would she think, I wondered, if I were to tell her my story? I was feeling recklessly happy and relaxed with the rhythm of the engine as we pulled out of the station. Stephen would be surprised to see me again so soon. I felt almost embarrassed. But I had a good enough reason for coming, I reassured myself.

It was nearly lunch-time when I arrived. I had forgotten it was Sunday and surveyed the closed shops indignantly. At last, I found a small dairy which was open, and bought a packet of potato crisps and some chocolate. At two o'clock I was standing, hesitant, outside No. 21 Woodlands Way, my hand on the gate. The street was empty and the small semi-detached houses had a withdrawn look. Straightening my scarf, I followed a crack in the concrete path, up to the red-brick porch. The door opened before I had had time to ring the bell, and I was confronted by a girl in jeans and a black sweater, smiling broadly. She laughed at my surprised expression.

'I saw you from the window. It is Diana, isn't it? Yes, Stephen said he ran into you yesterday. You haven't changed, you know. Hardly at all. Have I?'

'Well—no. Just older-looking.'

'Well, thank you. It's one of my first ambitions—to be sophisticated. Jim says I never will. Jim's my old faithful. He thinks he's known me long enough to be insulting. Maureen!'

A rather severe-looking girl appeared at the head of the stairs, holding a bottle of ink in her hand.

'It's Diana. Hasn't she not changed? Oh,' in disgust, 'you're not still working?'

'No, I was writing a letter. It can wait. How are you, Diana?'

'Very well, thank you.' Her manner made me feel suddenly shy.

'What do you think of England now that you're back?' she asked, as we followed Kathleen into the living-room.

'It's changed a lot, of course.' I felt around for sure ground.

'Yes, they've cut down the woods at the top of the road and put up council houses. Isn't it sickening?'

Kathleen broke in. 'Of course, there's always the common. You liked the common, didn't you?'

'Oh, yes.'

'Give me your coat. I'll put it in the bedroom.'

Kathleen turned to me as her sister left the room. 'Stephen will be sorry he missed you. He's staying the night over at Horley. What do you think of our Stephen, anyway?'

'Why, he——'

Kathleen rushed on. 'He's terribly irresponsible. I mean about a job and things. It worries Maureen awfully. She worries about both of us.'

'What does he do?' I pursued.

'Stephen? Well, he started off at Birkbeck—all set to get a Ph.D., but some girl took his mind off that and he missed his first exams. So then he branched out in agriculture, of all things, but he soon got bored with that. And now he's teaching at Salfords school—Standard Two. Talk about *Hurry On Down*. Have you read that book? John Wain. Haven't you? But you read an awful lot, don't you? Or used to?'

'Yes, but I don't belong to the library at the moment. I've been waiting to see where I'd get a job.' I said this rather hurriedly.

'Are you looking for one? What sort of job? I worked last holidays—there's an agency at Reigate. . . .'

'Stephen said Maureen knew a friend who had an agency.'

'Yes, that's the one. Maureen'll tell you where to go. She loves doing little maps.'

'I what?' Maureen came back with a laden tray.

'You love doing little maps. Diana wants to know how to get to that agency—you know, Doreen's.'

'Oh, yes, you're looking for a job.' Maureen nodded. 'Did you want one near here then? Stephen said you had a good place to live in London.'

'Well, that's just the trouble. I've just been told that the man who had my room before me is coming back.'

'Then p'raps a live-in job would be the thing? We'd love to have you here, but we've only the two bedrooms now. Stephen turned the third into a dark-room.'

'Yes, I wouldn't mind a live-in job at all,' I said hurriedly. 'Are they easy to get?'

'Oh, yes, they're the easiest,' Kathleen broke in.

'Of course, you don't earn as much, but you don't need to. You get your board, and that's the main thing. P'raps you were trying to save for your trousseau, though?'

'Well, I was. But Mummy's bought me quite a few things, anyway.' I hoped this didn't sound as if I had been spoilt. Perhaps I had. I half smiled to myself.

'Oh, in America, you mean? When are they coming to England, do you know?' Maureen asked.

'Well, she was rather vague in her last letter,' I said, hoping this didn't sound too feeble. I added: 'I don't think it'll be long now, though.'

'What sort of work did you do in the holidays?' I asked Kathleen later on.

'Oh, on a farm. That was summer of course. It was wonderful.'

'Oh, yes, you love horses, don't you?' I surprised myself by saying.

Kathleen gave a deep sigh. 'Remember old Pip? I had to give him up when we moved here—I cried and cried. That was the day I was confirmed, and everyone thought I was terribly moved by the service.' She giggled.

'Oh, Kath, you are awful!' Maureen thrust a plate of biscuits towards me. 'Look, you will stay on for dinner, won't you, Diana? It seems a shame to rush all that way back to London.'

'Well, yes—thank you very much.'

'Oh good.' Kathleen sprang up. 'Then you'll have time to see my sketches. I've nearly papered the walls with them. We'll leave Maureen to write her letter. Call us when you want some help with dinner,' she added over her shoulder to her sister.

'This is our bedroom.' Kathleen pushed open the door at the top of the stairs. 'It's dreadful sleeping with Maureen. She doesn't snore, but she grates her teeth. And she gets mad if I put on the light in the night, to write down an idea I've had for a sketch or something. I'm just dying for her to get married.' She glanced at me, and I laughed rather feebly. 'I think she's trying to get me off her hands first, though. Of course, the house would go to rack and ruin with just Stephen and I. It's Uncle's house really. He rents it to us for practically nothing, and that's not exaggerating. You're engaged though, aren't you? Tell me all about him.'

I felt a sudden urge to confide in her, to pour out intimate secrets and see how she would revel in them. Unfortunately I could think of very little to say. 'Well, he's dark, not very tall, not very handsome——' I began, 'but I think he's interesting.'

'Oh, he must be, if he's not handsome!'

'And he's rather irresponsible. Like Stephen I suppose.'

'Oh, I'm so glad. That's just what Jim isn't.' She looked rueful. 'He's terribly reliable. And another thing—he thinks my paintings are queer!'

I tried to look shocked. I had been surreptitiously studying the daubed sheets of paper pinned to the walls and thinking them decidedly odd. Kathleen had noticed my gaze.

'Of course, they're supposed to be queer—but in a certain way. I think I've got the right kind of queerness, in most of them, anyway. They're not too queer to understand. You do think he sounds horrid, don't you?'

'Well, I'd like to meet him first,' I laughed. I was still fascinated by the paintings. They were done in startling water-colours and she seemed very fond of that new colour, red. I pointed this out.

'Oh, yes. Once I painted a whole picture in different shades of red. Even Stephen liked it—he said it was so horrible you couldn't help liking it. I think he gave it to his girl friend to symbolize his feelings for her or something. Of course, that was ages ago, before I went to art school.'

'Do you really like art school?' I asked her.

'Oh, it's heaven! One of the masters is awfully nice.' She

paused dreamily. 'Do you know what he said once? He said I should get drunk. It would do my inhibitions good.'

'So you've got some?' I couldn't help saying. I was beginning to feel curiously at home.

'Oh, I've got a simply dreadful lot. They think I'm such a prude at school. But I'm looking forward to getting rid of them. I don't like drink though, except champagne. And no one ever buys me champagne. I think I'd paint a wonderful picture when I was drunk. I have such lovely ideas when I'm asleep, but when I wake up and try to do something about it, it goes all fishy.'

I found myself laughing quite naturally.

'I suppose Maureen takes life much more seriously,' I said later on.

'Oh, Maureen, yes. She feels responsible for all of us. And she's terribly keen at her job too. How anyone could be keen about secretarial work—beats me. She didn't used to be so bad—only since Dad died, you know. Though she always used to be a bit of a "mother" to us. Stephen didn't take too kindly to it. They're always at each other's throats. Stephen's got a hell of a temper. That reminds me—he couldn't stop telling us how pretty you'd got. You have, too.'

I was beginning to blush, when Maureen's voice came up the stairs.

'O.K., you can do the spuds now, Kathleen. It's my turn to talk to Diana.'

We went downstairs.

6

THE next day I visited the agency Maureen had directed me to. It meant another train journey, but it would be worth it if I could get a job in Redhill or somewhere near the Bartletts. I left early so as to avoid an encounter with Mrs Reid. It had been colder than ever in the night, and I was wearing some rather scuffed looking fur boots, which I had discovered at the back of my wardrobe.... In spite of the late hour at which I'd arrived back the night before, I had felt too excited to sleep, so had spent the best part of two hours packing up my things in readiness to leave, when I decided where I was going.

Now I stumped along Victoria Station, noticing happily that my surroundings had an already familiar aspect. This new adaptability in myself was something I had noticed only recently. It pleased me, because it made life more comfortable, although at the back of my mind a horror of change still lurked.

The agency wasn't difficult to find. When I left by the little back stairs, to come into the high street again, I was tingling with a sense of well being. Everything was arranged, Maureen's friend had sorted out a job as 'mother's help'.

with 'a very nice family'. They had two children, a girl of four and a baby of eighteen months.

'Do you like children?'

'Oh, yes,' I had agreed swiftly. The agent had rung Mrs Muir and made me an appointment with her that afternoon. It only remained for me to present myself with the reference Maureen had given me, and make a good impression. I looked down at my scuffed boots, and my spirits dropped a little. My coat was slightly grubby too, and it had shrunk out of shape at the back, which gave me rather an odd profile. I glared at the shop window which had pointed out these things, then gave a brief laugh. I was too happy to let little things upset me.

After a big lunch in a milk-bar, I caught the bus to the address in Horley which the agent had given me. The Muirs' house was large and rambling, at the end of a neglected driveway. I looked at the heavy knocker with some apprehension before raising it. The door was opened by a young woman in a tight, wool frock, who held out her hand to me in a straightforward manner.

'Miss Clouston? Come in. We're not terribly tidy yet, I'm afraid. We only moved in a few days ago, and I expect you know what that means.'

I followed her into the front room, where a fire was burning fitfully in the grate.

'I suppose the agent has told you what I required in the way of a girl? We send the heavy washing out to the laundry, so there's just the household chores, plus a bit of help with the children. No cooking—except perhaps if you could manage the breakfast now and then. We've got an Aga which we stoke up to last right through till morning.' She looked at me. 'What do you think? Does it sound as if it would suit you?' She read my letter of reference through, with a slightly over-casual air, and said brightly: 'Yes, that seems all right. I don't know what you expected in the way of wages, though. I'm afraid we're not in a position to pay you very much at present. What I had in mind was somewhere about two pound five?'

I assured her this would suit me very well, and she led me out to show me briefly over the house.

'I don't think it's a bad house to keep clean. It's smaller than what we're used to, out in the country, and you see we've had the kitchen renovated. That really was in a mess. This is the children's play-room. I don't expect you to keep this very tidy.' She gave a low chuckle. 'Wazzie, this is Miss Clouston.'

'Diana,' I interrupted quickly.

'Well, Diana then, if you don't mind. This is Wendolin. We call her Wazzie, I'm afraid. And Baby John is sleeping in his pram.'

I moved in the following day. Leaving Cadogan Square had given me a fresh feeling of elation. For the first time I understood the cliché 'on the crest of a wave'. I was riding the biggest wave imaginable, and where it would deposit me was one of the mysteries I required no answer to at the time. I had paid Mrs Reid my rent up to date, and found I could still afford a taxi to the train with my two cases. With the memory of the shabby little room behind me, I seemed to have discarded the atmosphere of perilous security and doubt of my own sanity. Everything ahead of me was homely, safe and comfortable, as Mrs Muir's freckled face. I was determined that from now on I would enjoy life for its own sake, and not examine it too closely or brood on my memories of Micald. I had been given a new identity. I would enjoy it in my own way.

At least half of my well-being could, I suppose, have been bed to the taxi I was relaxing in. This was a luxury for me, and at the end of the trip I tipped the driver rather furtively, hobbling away with my cases.

The room I was given at Top Lodge, as the house was called, was large and draughty, with bare skirting boards and very little furniture. However, a big, soft eiderdowned bed commanded the centre of one wall, and there was ample wardrobe space for my few clothes. Mrs Muir left me to unpack, while she went to fetch Waz home from the nearby day school. I arranged my clothes and possessions in the drawers, with a warm glow of pleasure at my own tidiness. I had just pushed the cases under the bed when, through the window, I saw Mrs Muir returning with Wendolin in a small maroon school uniform.

That night I had dinner with Mrs Muir and her husband in the lounge. She had said to me earlier:

'Normally you can have high tea with the children, and then we'll leave you dinner in the oven so you can help yourself later on. But tonight, as Mr Muir would like to see you, we thought you could have it with us.' She seemed faintly embarrassed, and all I could do was look embarrassed in return. It didn't occur to me to thank her.

But as we sat in front of the fire, helping ourselves from a tea-wagon to macaroni cheese and fish pie, I felt myself responding willingly to their polite cross-examination of me. Mr Muir was a big, ginger-moustached man, with a rather affected voice. He was fond of making puns, then looking exaggeratedly shamefaced. Mrs Muir tried to keep the conversation serious, and soon I began to feel, with some amusement, that she thought of me as ever so slightly dumb. In reply to a question about my parents, I suddenly surprised both of us by saying:

'Well, my father's a Doctor of Philosophy. He's in America on his sabbatical leave at the moment, with my mother. They're coming to England some time soon though.'

There was a startled silence, then Mrs Muir said: 'Oh, and are you interested in philosophy too?'

'No, I don't understand much about it. I tried to read Daddy's books when I was too young and I think it put me off.'

We returned to talk of other things, but later on Mrs Muir said suddenly:

'What made you think of taking on a job like this?'

'I don't know,' I smiled at her. 'I suppose I thought it would be a change. And then I liked the idea of a live-in job.'

'Well, I hope you don't tire of it in too much of a hurry. Most of your evenings will be your own, except when we want to go out.' She was looking vaguely worried.

'Perhaps Diana would like a glass of sherry with us,' said Mr Muir.

.   .   .   .   .

The rest of the week passed swiftly enough, and I found myself enjoying the routine life in this family atmosphere. Mr Muir knocked on my door early each morning to wake me, and I would doze for a few minutes more before bouncing out of bed and dressing frantically, on the cold linoleum in front of the dressing-table. I would arrive downstairs with crooked lipstick, and tying my white apron, which was too big for me, and had to be tucked in the middle. Before long, warm coffee fumes would steam up around my eyes—always the coldest part of me, and thaw them back into focus. Wendolin was the most difficult to please.

'Mummy does the sausages in flour.'

'That will do, Wazzie,' from Mrs Muir.

'Oh, you've put Marmite! I said marmalade!'

'Well, give it to Baby John,' I would croak in my raw, morning voice.

As I swept and polished, I would keep one ear on the radio, which was very rarely switched off. The popular songs surprised and often bewildered me. Those I had been used to were far more intelligible, but curiously monotonous. I soon found myself humming over the sink. As Mrs Muir had promised, most of my evenings after six were free. I would clear the children's tea, which I gave them at four o'clock, then we would sit in the warm lounge, reading stories by a table-lamp. Before six Mrs Muir would help me bath them, and after that my time was my own.

It was cold, sitting up in my room, but sometimes I would borrow the play-room heater and toast one leg at a time as I sprawled on the mat. I had joined the local library, one day out shopping with the children, and now had plenty to read. What had fascinated me was a book of poems by W. H. Auden. Mrs Muir had looked rather surprised at my selection of books, and it wasn't till some time later that I discovered poetry wasn't read by the masses as it was in Micald. I soon realized why. Poetry in Micald was much more everyday, readable matter. It was no more difficult to understand than prose—prose on a slightly elevated level. And yet, as I let

W. H. Auden creep into my sleepy, ten o'clock brain, I felt curiously moved, without fully understanding why. The strange thing was that it had a familiar flavour to it. Before long I could have sworn I had known of the existence of such poetry all my life. It was after a late night, reading this disturbing book, that I woke feeling restless for the first time since starting work. Mr Muir was knocking firmly on my door, and he called out:

'Better hurry if you're coming to Mass.'

I brightened immediately and remembered that Mrs Muir had offered to prepare the breakfast, while I went to church with Mr Muir.

'I'll go to the eleven o'clock Mass with the children,' she had explained.

Now I dressed quickly and followed Mr Muir out to the station-wagon, nibbling a banana in place of breakfast. He drove recklessly, and I was pleased to be able to relax in the dim, almost silent church. The service disappointed me, because I found I could understand so little of it. It was conducted in a language similar to one spoken in a country across the sea from Micald, but which I had never studied. This turned my mind to think of what countries existed beyond England, other than America and New Zealand. I had been lacking in knowledge of geography, back in Micald. Here I would be considered almost moronically ignorant, if I didn't find an atlas and study it, thoroughly and soon. I made a note to borrow one from the library, and couldn't help smiling at the idea of what Mrs Muir's expression might be. She thought my tastes odd enough as it was. But now people were getting up and leaving the church. Mr Muir said to me quietly:

'Go out to the car. I'll be there in a few minutes.'

I left the church, watching inquisitively as the shuffling file of people crossed themselves briefly with holy water. Sitting in the front seat of the station-wagon, waiting for Mr Muir, the mysterious odour and atmosphere of the church remained with me. It made me feel slightly uncomfortable, and reminded me of my feeling of dread and claustrophobia, which had made me leave the church near Cadogan Square in such a hurry. I wondered, for the first time, if I really wanted to have anything to do with this religion. Its mysteriousness made me feel insecure. Mr Muir returned, and we drove back in silence.

That day we had a midday roast dinner in the dining-room, with Mr Muir making jokes and playing with Wendolin's feet under the table.

'When am I having my birthday, Mummy?' she asked suddenly, picking up a square of Yorkshire pudding.

'Put that down and use your fork, or you won't be having one.'

'Mark's coming to my party, isn't he? Who else is coming?'

'Who would you like?'

'Elena. Elena doesn't know we've got a new maid, does she?'

'Waz! Diana isn't our maid. Now wait while I wipe your fingers. You are a messy girl. Look at Baby John.'

'Well, you feed him. Anyway, he's usually worse than that. Throw your meat out, John.'

'I'll smack you, Wendolin.'

Wendolin squirmed down in her chair and pulled a face. I listened to this conversation with half an ear. Mrs Muir had paid me the night before, and I was thinking of how I would spend the following evening, if the Muirs weren't planning to go out. She had said to me several times: 'I believe there's a good film on in Horley. Isn't there someone you could go with?'

I had thought of Kathleen. I had thought of Josie. I had even thought of Stephen. It occurred to me that I should be doing something to keep in touch with these people. It would be a pity not to see Kathleen again. I felt as if I knew her quite well. Perhaps we had corresponded while I was in New Zealand. This reminded me of Robert. I had had one letter from him, sent on from Cadogan Square, and his earnest: *Darling, why haven't you written? Are you all right? Please, please write soon. I'm praying to hear from you*, had made me feel guilty. I made up my mind to write that night. It would be easier now that I had something to tell him—about my visit to the Bartletts and my new job.

That evening the Muirs went next door for cocktails and I was able to spend the evening in the warm-carpeted lounge. Baby John was wakeful and disturbing Wendolin, so I put him in the pram beside the fire with me, and quietened him occasionally with a peppermint. Sprawled with the sweet-bag open alongside me, I composed my letter. I hoped Robert wouldn't notice that my writing was bigger than his own, and that I didn't quite write to the edges of the air-letter form. At the bottom I wrote: *Darling, I love you—very much.*

I felt sick, and crunched down hard on my peppermint.

7

IT WAS only the following Tuesday morning, when I was punching up the cushions in the lounge and raking out the grate, that the letter from Maureen came. It was an invitation to her twenty-fourth birthday party on the following Saturday. I stuffed the letter in my apron pocket and went on raking out the fire. Nevertheless, I was excited, and a sense of expectation warmed the rest of the day for me.

I supposed that parties here were celebrated in the same way that I was used to, but the different climate made me doubtful about what I should wear. I dare not ask Mrs Muir and show what, to her, would seem unnecessary ignorance. Then I thought of the one taffeta frock that was hanging in my wardrobe, and decided I would take a chance and wear it. It was plain but inoffensive, and didn't look too cold. There would be the question of a present, too. It would have to be something inexpensive, because I'd spent a good part of my wages already on books.

The day before Mr Muir had driven his wife and Wendolin up to London for the day, and I had spent the afternoon wheeling Baby John around the shops, doing a few messages. I had taken this opportunity to buy two fairly elementary school books on history and geography. At the same time

I had bought a thick diary with a collection of general information in the front pages. During the school days, I could remember, I had never been very keen on studying for the various exams. Now, however, I found it satisfying in an unfamiliar way, and would absorb each fact with the delicate enjoyment of a gourmet sampling new dishes.

Coming back to the present, I gathered the two empty sherry glasses into my hand, balanced them on an ash-tray and made my way to the kitchen.

'Something nice?' Mrs Muir asked later, as I read the letter for a second time, with pink hands straight from the washing-up.

'Yes,' I told her.

'Oh, that is nice for you. I don't suppose you've been to many parties since you got here—have you?'

I smiled at her obvious curiosity. 'Not one, I'm afraid.'

'It will be a change then, won't it? Wazzie's party will be coming very soon. Are you good at children's parties? They can be such horrible affairs if you don't plan every little thing. We'll have to clear the play-room. There'll only be a handful of other kiddies. She gets excited so easily. And your thing's on Saturday, you say?'

On Saturday I ironed my frock in the kitchen and dressed carefully, shivering a little with cold and excitement. In the bus I took out Maureen's present and looked at it thoughtfully. It was a writing set, from a chain-store, in cheap imitation leather, and now I noticed that the fern pattern on the front was slightly askew. I had been quite surprised at the low price of it, and of the other goods on sale at this store. All the same, I had not realized at the time that Maureen would guess where her present had been purchased. I had never come across the phenomenon of the cheap chain-store in Micald. Prices had varied little from shop to shop. In spite of my ignorance, however, a faint inkling of doubt about my choice of the present worried me. Thinking of this, I looked up to see the grey police station at the foot of the Bartletts' street, and scrambled off the bus just before it started up again.

By the time I reached the doorway of number twenty-one, my face and hands were stiff and raw from the cold wind. Maureen opened the door to me and herded me into the front room with a bright introduction. Kathleen was propped against the mantelpiece, in a bright green dress, and jumped up to greet me.

'This is Jim,' she told me on a lower note, and indicated a round-jawed youth with a slight cast in one eye. I told her how nice she was looking.

'Gosh, you should have seen me this morning,' she said, 'rushing round burning scones and things. And Maureen was madly hunting out games from a feeble book she picked up somewhere. I hate games at a party, don't you? Except for "Murders". We'll be playing "Murders" later on. And Stephen slunk off to the football, as usual. Not the football—the slinking off, I mean. I don't know what made him go to football this week. Just a chance to get away from all our panic I suppose. Anyway, how about the job? Do you like it?'

'Yes, I do really. They're very nice people. The little girl's a bit of a handful,' I told her.

'How old?'

'Four and a half. She's always encouraging her baby brother to be naughty, and he's catching on quite well.'

'I suppose she'll moan about keeping him to the straight and narrow when he's grown up a bit. That reminds me. Where's Stephen?'

'At the bar,' Jim interposed, pointing to a wooden bureau well stocked with bottles and glasses.

'Of course, he's barman. Oh, Jim, we are awful. Here's Diana with nothing to drink. What would you like? The punch is nice and potent. I made it myself.' She slipped across the room to fetch me a glass. Stephen glanced up and waved. Later on, in a lull between games, he came over and sat beside me.'

'Hallo. Enjoying yourself?'

'Very much.'

'Not in a daze tonight I hope.' He grinned. 'You *were* in a funny mood that night.'

'Was I?'

'Yes. Well, you may always be like that—I wouldn't know —but you look different tonight somehow.'

'Yes, I feel different. I think London had a bad effect on me.' I smiled.

'You like your job then?'

'Yes, I do, as a matter of fact.'

'I didn't think girls liked domestic chores, unless it was their own household they were running.'

'No—well, I don't know why, but I like it. The two kids are quite amusing.'

'It's more than I can say for my job.' He looked rueful. 'Of course, the kids *are* amusing sometimes, but more often they're just plain little blighters. How's your glass?'

'Very nice, thank you. I never drink fast. What's this stuff in it?' I queried.

'Mint. Don't worry, it's not an insect,' he grinned.

'Oh, I know.' I looked down in embarrassment and took a quick gulp.

'Well, I'd better get circulating.' He stood up and began to move away.

'Is everybody ready? I'm going to deal the cards for "Murders",' Maureen shouted, and the noise of conversation rattled away to silence.

For a moment a touch of fear chilled me at the grim associations of the word. In the homely atmosphere of the Muir household I had almost forgotten the frequent crimes reported in the newspapers. At least, I had decided that they confined themselves mainly to the newspapers and had nothing to do with myself and friends. Unconsciously I had arrived quickly at a fallacy held by many people who had been in this world a lot longer than I had. Looking at the glowing, amused faces around me, I felt the chill of fear die quickly.

'Ace is murderer, King is judge,' Maureen was saying as she dealt the cards around briskly. She went on to explain how the game was played, although most of the guests seemed already familiar with it.

I turned over my card and was confronted with the Jack of Spades. At least I wouldn't have to do any 'murdering', myself. Relieved, I followed the others off to hide in the darkened rooms of the house. There was a silence, broken only by an occasional giggle as someone bumped into someone else. A moment of fearful expectancy—then suddenly a pair of warm hands clasped my neck lightly and fell away again. I screamed, a genuine scream of terror, and in that moment I half turned and saw it was Stephen. He was laughing at me, and his teeth were a white line in the moonlight. Then he had disappeared, and the lights went on.

I flung myself, rather late, into a 'murdered' attitude on the floor. I was discovered with appropriate cries of horror and the trial was begun. It didn't take long for the judge to pick out Stephen as the murderer, and I suddenly realized that the game always followed the same inevitable pattern. Where was the enjoyment supposed to lie? In the horror of waiting for hands to descend in the darkness? In the opportunity to frighten someone into a scream, and not have it treated seriously? I 'came to life', and glanced across at Stephen as I stretched a cramped leg. He was laughing silently again, and his teeth were still white. I wondered how it was I had never noticed them before. I think I was staring rather foolishly, but I forced myself into a smile and he came over to me.

'Did I frighten you?'

'You certainly did.' I was relieved to be able to talk about it.

'You didn't come across "Murders" in New Zealand?' he asked.

'I can't say I remember it.'

'Well, keep on the move next time and you won't be such a likely victim. It *is* a mad game, but it's been a sort of tradition at our parties.'

We accepted cards for a second round. It was soon after this that I discovered a tiny rash on my arms and throat.

'Look! I've gone spotty all of a sudden,' I confided to Kathleen. She stared at me for a moment, then burst out laughing.

'Stephen, look what you've done to this poor girl! She's come out in a nervous rash all over!'

'Do you think that's what it is?' I asked doubtfully.

'Good heavens!' Stephen lifted up an arm and examined it. He looked at me quizzically, and suddenly I noticed how attractive his eyes were.

'It could be measles,' Jim said in a flat, solid voice.

'Goodness——' I began. 'No, but I haven't felt sick or anything. I feel quite marvellous.'

'It's a nervous rash,' Kathleen insisted. And it appeared she was right, for it had gone completely by the time the party was breaking up. It was after one o'clock, and Stephen offered to drive me home in his little Austin.

'Not very elegant, I'm afraid,' he said, pulling a tuft of loose stuffing out of the passenger seat. 'However, she goes like a bomb and that's the main thing.'

I crawled in out of the cold night air, and he shut the door with a clatter. 'Have you been to see the old school—St Johns —yet?' he asked warming up the engine.

'No, I'm afraid I haven't.'

'Oh good, we can—oh blast!' The engine had stopped. 'Look, why don't we have a look at it tonight? I just start living at this hour.' We bumped off down the road.

'But—how——?' I was going to ask how far it was, but stopped myself in time. That was something I should evidently know already.

Stephen laughed at my stuttering. 'Well, look, if you're tired——'

'Oh, I'm not tired,' I said hurriedly. 'Do you really want to?'

'Of course. Come on. I'll show you how she performs on the sewerage dump hill.'

He stopped the car at the foot of a concrete slope and

handed me out. 'Of course, it'll be locked, but you're not interested in the inside, are you? I can tell you it hasn't changed much. I taught here for about six weeks, relieving.'

'Oh, I remember this!' I exclaimed involuntarily as we came into the playground.

'Of course you do.'

'No, but I mean—it's just the same,' I added quickly.

'Hey, you're not cold, are you?' he asked, as I drew my coat in closer.

'Well, I'm not roasting,' I admitted.

'Come out of the wind a minute.' He led me into a shelter shed and sat me on a form. 'It's not too warm either. Gosh, it's a long time since I sat here and ate my lunch. I was down in the boys' school, wasn't I, by the time you came here?'

'That's right.'

'You know, I don't remember you all that well—just someone small and fluffy with big eyes.'

'I suppose I've changed a lot,' I laughed.

'Oh, yes. Remember that little red leather coat you had? I do remember that.'

'I've got a vague recollection.'

'Oh, but yes, of course you've changed. You used to be pretty—now you're extremely attractive.'

I didn't know what to say.

'You don't think your fiancé would object to my paying you compliments?'

I couldn't help giving a short laugh.

'Why, what's funny?'

'Nothing. Yes, he's terribly possessive.' I noticed that I said this rather contemptuously.

'I suppose he writes screeds of letters?' Stephen pursued.

'I'm afraid he does. It makes me guilty because I can't write screeds back. I try, but nothing much happens to tell him about.'

'Oh surely—is life so dull? Why not make something happen? You sound a bit disillusioned. What are you—eighteen?'

'Nineteen—just.'

'I suppose you believe in young marriages?'

'Definitely.'

'Of course, you're a woman. Well, a girl. Are you madly in love? No, don't bother. I'm always rude like this. I can't help wondering, though, how you could bring yourself to leave him for—a year, isn't it?—you mean to stay?'

'About that, yes. Well, I wanted to have a last fling——'

'Yes, I could have believed that till I met you. You seem to have grown into a very subdued, responsible girl. I see no signs of a last fling.'

'Neither do I,' I said rather quietly. I was realizing that this was what I should have been doing while I was in London—what, in fact, I was expected to be doing.

'Did your fiancé like the idea of a last fling?' Stephen grinned down at me.

'Well, naturally, I promised it would be harmless.'

'I suppose he's having a last fling of his own at the same time?'

'Oh, I doubt it. He doesn't sound—I mean, he isn't really the type. Terribly faithful and all that. Ooph, I'm freezing! Let's get moving again, shall we?'

'Oh, yes, all right. I suppose we'd better see the common another day. It's a bit wintry.'

We were silent going down the slope. Outside Top Lodge

he put his hand on my shoulder. 'Look, I'll help you with that last fling—harmless, naturally——' His white teeth flashed. 'Let's make it pictures next Friday. Can you get away from the offspring?'

'Yes, I think so. Thank you, it would be lovely.'

'Good. I'll pick you up.'

8

It was amazing how much pleasure I got out of that one picture of his white teeth smiling a kind of delicious threat. It would come to me several times a day—banging the mats on the line, dusting the brass ornaments which hung from the wall—and my bones seemed to shrink inside me. He took me to the local cinema that Friday to see *Black Widow*. The whole film stands out in my mind with extraordinary clearness—and this is surprising, because my eyes kept flickering to the curly head leaning back beside me. He had taken my hand in the picture queue, with a sudden, self-conscious movement, and we had avoided each other's eyes. Now, however, he was smoking, slowly and deeply, with his long, brown fingers curled round a stubby holder. I noticed his nostrils pinch and dilate as he drew each breath, and it had a curiously hypnotizing effect on me.

We talked for a long time afterwards, sitting in the draughty car. I remember I was fiddling with a chain which drew the door handle down, and finally broke it. Stephen laughed and said it was never any use, anyway.

'I don't think your nerves can be very good,' he went on. 'By the way, you don't smoke, do you?'

'No.' I watched the thin smoke curl away from his white

teeth. I wondered if he cleaned them with baking soda makes me sick,' I explained.

'Good girl. It's damned expensive, anyway.'

I discovered there was plenty I could talk about without showing excessive ignorance, as long as the conversation remained general. As soon as Stephen began to illustrate his remarks with quotations and proper names, I tried to steer the conversation on to something else. I even found myself enjoying this. At the same time I realized it couldn't go on indefinitely and was prepared to do something about it. Already I had bought two books on artists and composers, and a survey of English literature. I hadn't had much opportunity yet to study them, but what I had read I didn't find difficult to remember. It was as if I were merely revising knowledge I had learnt previously, it was so very easy to absorb. So, although I had so much to catch up on, I didn't think of this as an overwhelming task. On the contrary, it was all part of an adventure. I was getting drowsy when Stephen lay his arm across my shoulder, and I glanced up so quickly that he looked startled, and said briskly:

'Have you been up to London at all since you got this job?'

'No, I haven't,' I told him. 'I was just thinking, I should have gone up last night to a lecture at the Grail. I'd been going to them.'

He looked at me blankly, so I went on:

'Robert's a Catholic, you see.'

'Oh, is that it?' He looked faintly embarrassed. 'I suppose he's been trying to convert you?'

'I suppose you'd call it that.'

He paused, then: 'Maureen's got a thing about Catholics.'

'You mean she doesn't like them?'

'I mean she doesn't like them.'

'What do you think?' I asked, pleased that I had found someone to discuss it with.

'Of course, everybody's entitled to their own religion. Personally, I haven't got one. It's much easier. I've never studied the Roman Catholic religion particularly. But I wouldn't like to be involved in it.'

'You don't think I should change to be a—Catholic?'

'Mixed marriages are a mess, more often than not. Still, I don't think you should turn purely on those grounds. You've just got yourself in a difficult position.'

'I have, haven't I?' I was only now realizing its difficulties.

'Why not forget about him?' he said jokingly. 'Must be plenty of nice atheists around.'

I was wishing fervently that I could.

The next afternoon I met with a series of shocks. I had been dusting the lounge when the telephone rang beside my hand, and I lifted it expecting another business friend of Mr Muir's. However, the voice at the other end asked to speak to me.

'Oh, hallo, Diana,' she went on. 'It's Maureen here. Hold the line, your boy friend wants to speak to you.'

A picture of Stephen flashed into my mind, but a deep masculine voice was already greeting me.

'Hallo, Di, dear. It's Daddy.'

'Oh, Daddy!' I gasped, and a cold shudder ran right over my scalp.

'Yes, I thought I'd surprise you. We got passages at short notice. I supposed you'd be busy working, so I thought I'd better ring and see when it would be best to come around. The Bartletts have kindly asked me to tea.'

'Where's Mummy?' I asked timidly.

'Oh, she can't come ashore till morning. She's on the *Queen Mary*. I flew, you see. I've just driven up from London in a new Ford Prefect I bought this morning.'

'Bought?' I was too bewildered to worry about the impression I was making.

He gave a deep, happy laugh. 'Yes, that's right. Goodness, Di, it's a whale of a job finding your way out of London. I got on to the wrong road twice.'

'And where are you staying?' I had thought of the two bedrooms in the Bartletts' house.

'At the Feathers at Merstham—you know, where we were before. Aunty Edna booked for us. Apparently she didn't know about your job.'

'No, I'm afraid I haven't written. Did she say anything?'

'She seemed to think she was the one who should write to you.'

'Oh, that's all right then.'

'Well, can I manage to see you tonight?'

'Oh dear—I'm dying to see you, Daddy, but—I just thought —Mrs Muir's having a bit of a party tonight, and she expected me to help with it. I'll ask her, shall I?'

'Oh, no, no, no. I'll see you tomorrow. And Mummy can come over with me. Will tomorrow be all right?'

'Yes, of course—but I could probably see you for a short time tonight.'

'No, don't worry about it. Mustn't get you in bad with your employers. Are they nice people?'

'Yes, very. Gosh, I was bowled over, hearing your voice like that. I'm just beginning to realize you're in England now.' I tried to sound a bit breathless with pleasure. When

I rang off, I sat down with the duster hanging from a trembling hand. I was relieved to think that I had twenty-four hours in which to compose myself. At the same time I was hoping I hadn't offended my father. He sounded a nice man, though very different from my father in Micald. I wondered if I were normally an affectionate daughter to him. He hadn't sounded offended, and of course my excuse was quite valid. I roused myself as Mrs Muir came into the room, and told her shyly of my 'phone call.

'He's coming round to see me—with my mother—tomorrow night. You didn't want me for anything, did you?'

'No, dear, that's quite all right. I suppose you're all excited. How long is it since you last saw them?'

'It's nearly a year now. They went to America before I left New Zealand. At least, they came here first, then went on to America.' I had gleaned this fact from something Maureen had said, and I hoped urgently that I hadn't made a mistake. It would be unfortunate if I got my facts wrong at this point.

'And now they're back here again. I see,' Mrs Muir nodded. 'They certainly get about, don't they?'

I was waiting at the top of the stairs when the doorbell rang the following evening. Mrs Muir came out of the lounge to go to the door, so I halted my footsteps until she had opened it. Then I ran quickly down the stairs and greeted my mother.

'Hallo, Disy, darling. Aren't you going to be kissed?' She pulled my cheek round towards her, then gave an embarrassed laugh in Mrs Muir's direction. 'I suppose she's shy after not seeing me so long.'

'Will you have a drink with us?' Mrs Muir smiled doubtfully.

'Well, that's very kind of you, but her Daddy's waiting out in the car. We thought we'd take her back to the hotel so she could see the things we've brought her back from America. I'm sure she's dying to see them. You know what young girls are like about clothes.' She tucked her fur coat collar under her chin as she turned back towards the door, and I followed her eager little steps across the drive. She was small and young-looking, with smooth, brown hair pulled back loosely in a bun. My mother in Micald had been bigger built, and her voice had been lower pitched, but her manner had been much the same, so I didn't feel as strange as I had feared I might.

We reached the car, and the first glimpse I had of my father was of the moonlight on his black-rimmed glasses. Then he leant across to open the door, and I saw a dark, square face with a slightly protruding jaw.

'Well, what do you think of her?' he asked.

'I—oh, the car, you mean. Very nice,' I responded.

'Better than the old Standard, eh?'

'You're telling me.'

We turned out on to the night road.

'You're looking a bit peaky. I hope you've been looking after yourself.' My mother looked back over her shoulder.

'Oh, Mummy.' The word seemed to fit and fasten on to her quite easily.

'Well, I know what you're like—always forgetting when you ate last, and keeping such irregular hours.'

'Oh, I keep very regular hours now. Out of necessity,' I told her.

'Oh, do they work you very hard, dear?' She sounded concerned.

'Not really. I just don't like getting up in the mornings, that's all.'

'Well, you haven't changed much in that direction.'

'The kids are rather sweet.' And I went on talking about my job with surprising ease and volubility.

'You'll be able to write a book about it, in the Monica Dickens style,' my father suggested.

I gave an incredulous laugh.

'Why? Don't you do any writing these days?' my mother asked in surprise.

'Not much, I'm afraid.' I was learning things about myself.

'Too busy writing letters, I suppose,' my father said teasingly.

'Yes, there's that of course,' I admitted. 'You can spend an awful lot of time on writing letters.'

'I do hope you like these things we've got for you,' my mother said, as we neared the hotel. 'It's hard to tell what someone else will like.'

'Oh, I'm sure I'll like them,' I assured her.

'Goodness, hasn't she got polite, Gerald?'

My father laughed. 'Oh, it'll wear off, dear. Don't let it worry you.'

We had reached the Feathers.

My parents' room was large and cold, with a small gas-fire burning low on one side of the room. I stood on the linoleum in my stockings and slip, trying on various articles of clothing. My mother searched these out from a big, shiny, brass trunk, and kept repeating:

'I don't remember what's in here, you know. It's so long since we packed it.'

'Oh, super!' I said. 'Smashing!' as I whirled round in a wide taffeta skirt.

'You like it?'

'Oh, yes.' I tried to sound eager and pleasantly surprised. It wasn't very difficult. 'I should have had this for Maureen's party,' I added, picking up a low-necked evening sweater.

'Oh, yes. Was it a good party, Di?'

'Lovely. We played "Murders". Oh, you must have spent pounds on all these.'

'Dollars, dear. Well, it's a pity that green one's too big, but we can take it in when we get home. You won't be wanting to wear it till then, will you?'

'No, I don't expect——' I sounded a little disappointed.

'Well, they're really for your trousseau, you know, but it's up to you if you want to wear them now. I suppose you're a bit low on clothes at the moment?' She uncurled her bun at the mirror, captured a loose strand, and curled it up again with a quick movement of her fingers.

'I must say I'm sick of this skirt and jumper. It's getting like a uniform.' I fastened the belt viciously.

'But haven't you got another skirt?'

'Yes, and another jumper. I alternate them. But it's still pretty dull.'

'Well, look, take these two winter frocks back with you. We'll probably get you some more later on.' She glanced across at my father as she said this, but he went on reading a magazine with a little frown splitting his wide forehead.

'Oh, thank you, Mummy. But don't bother getting any more. I should be able to save up.'

'You have changed, I must say.'

Yes, I must have been spoilt after all.

We went down to the lounge later on—a small, oddly shaped room, dimly lit and quite empty. We stood around the fireplace, where a surprisingly large fire burned noisily, and ate ham sandwiches brought by an ugly little maid.

'So you've given up the idea of a trip to Europe?' my father said quite suddenly.

Had I? Taken by surprise, I stared at him, and tried to look as if I was taking time to finish my bite before replying.

He was smiling in an amused fashion. 'London isn't the best place to save up money, is it?'

At once I realized what he meant. 'No, you're certainly right. I'll never save enough,' I agreed with him.

'Oh, Gerald, don't tease her,' my mother broke in. She turned to me. 'We've decided to take you with us, when we go on the Continent. Would you like that?'

'Oh, Mummy! That's wonderful.' I was taken aback, and must have looked it.

She gave a pleased laugh. 'Our finances are working out a little better than we expected. Of course, we'll have to go easy—find cheap hotels and so on.'

'What about my job?'

'Well, if you could get time off—but we'll be away six weeks. They'd probably have to get another girl.'

'Oh dear, I feel a bit awful—but I suppose they'll soon get someone else.'

'And you shouldn't have any trouble getting another job when you get back,' my father added. 'It wouldn't matter if it wasn't too wonderful, because you'd be coming home soon after that.'

'Yes,' I agreed thoughtfully, trying to sort out a gathering knot of confusion.

It was late when my father drove me home again, and I let myself into the silent house. I was feeling a little dizzy with tiredness and excitement. I was astonished at the ease with which I had fitted into the role of my new parents' daughter. Of course, they hadn't seen me for nearly a year, and any changes that had appeared in my character could well have developed in that time. Nevertheless, I couldn't help feeling a big hurdle had been jumped. Much too excited to sleep, I spent half the night studying maps of Europe, and some travel pamphlets which my mother had given me. Gradually the darkness seemed to be creeping into my eyes, and after a time I gave up trying to keep my heavy lids parted, and pulled the cord of my bedside lamp. It wasn't till morning that I thought again of Stephen.

9

HE RANG the following evening to ask me to a show up in London which he had tickets for.

'And so you're going on the Continent?' he added when there was a pause in the conversation.

'Oh, yes,' I began eagerly. 'How did you know?'

'Your father told us. Are you pleased about it? It would have been a shame not to, while you were over here, wouldn't it?'

'It would, yes. We're going in a couple of weeks. I've just broken the news to Mrs Muir. She's been awfully nice about it.' I lowered my voice, for she was in the next room.

'Mmm? I can't hear you. I've got a bit of a hangover. Went to a mad party last night.' He sounded depressed, so I said quickly:

'I'll be looking forward to the show on Friday. Thank you so much for asking me, Stephen.'

When I rang off I found some of Stephen's apparent depression had transferred itself to me. Upstairs in my bedroom I hunched my knees up in front of the fire and thought about the telephone conversation. Stephen had asked if I was pleased about going. Well, was I? It seemed fantastic to me that I should prefer not to go, merely so that I could visit a film with Stephen occasionally. As I've said before, I had never come up against someone I knew falling in love, in Micald, except in a very dull way. The idea that it could happen to me was even more unbelievable. And yet I couldn't help thinking of it now. After all, I was in a different world. Maybe falling in love was easy. Perhaps it could happen to a person more than once, and at the same time, like it had in a novel I had just finished.

A knot of pleasure swelled quickly in me, but was followed by a sudden uneasiness. It seemed more important than ever that Stephen should find my behaviour normal and natural. Up to now it had been easy to conceal that the life I remembered most clearly was of in another world. Would it remain easy? If I ever had to confess my story, he would think I was mad. It would be useless trying to convince him that it had really happened. For a moment an awful feeling came over me. There was no one I could really relax with and be comforted by. Even back in Micald it would be the same. I would always be sandwiched between two worlds, always acting, never sure which was the real me. Reaching out quickly for a pamphlet on Paris, I spread it on my knees and tried to read. But it was no use. Soon I lowered my head on to it and felt tears run across the paper.

. . . . .

We left for the Continent two weeks later. It all seems rather jumbled now—the trains, the foreign porters, my father frowning over the 'itinerary'. I wore my thick, pink coat and shabby boots, all the time while travelling, and carried a stubby umbrella with the head snapped off, threaded through the straps of my case. I took a lot of travel sickness pills, contrary to my mother's advice, and perhaps that accounts for the strange aura of confusion that surrounds my recollection of the whole six weeks. I remember one afternoon clearly, however, and for no particular reason.

We were staying at a spotlessly clean but extremely cold hotel in Belgium. There was a lot of dazzling white, and of bare, stained wood. The three of us had been given a room with a double and a single bed. Apparently this was considered quite respectable on the Continent. I lay on my white coverlet, in the sunlight, eating an orange, with sticky fingers, and reading my mail. Outside the streets were covered with hard snow, but the sun shone brazenly across the high rooftops. A rooster gargled into the quiet afternoon as I turned another page of my letter. I gave an indignant snort.

'What's the matter?' my mother asked, rubbing her stockinged feet where she lay on the other bed.

I had discovered by now, from Robert's letters, that his parents were particularly opposed to the match their son proposed to make. As far as I could make out it was on grounds that I was of a different religion, irresponsible, and possibly immoral. This had naturally raised a question in my mind. Was I a virgin any longer? I had felt myself blushing at the thought. At the same time I couldn't help smiling. Of course I was a virgin! Robert's indignation at his mother's accusations seemed clearly to point towards this. Now he was saying that perhaps we should put off our wedding another year, for on that condition only would his father help set him up in business, as he had promised. The snort had been driven from me by a sudden indignation that Robert should think I wanted to marry him, ever. This indignation was unreasonable, for I had done all I could to foster the illusion, in my letters to him. But the situation was beginning to irritate me.

'Just his silly parents,' I said to my mother. 'He thinks we should wait another year, in case they cut him off with a shilling.'

My mother hesitated, then said with a timid smile as though trying to make a joke of it: 'Do you think he really will marry you? Everything might seem different when you see each other again.'

For some reason this infuriated me. 'Oh, Mummy!' I spat a pip on to my saucer. 'Don't you start.' I wasn't quite sure what I meant, but it evidently didn't surprise her, because she dropped her eyes and began to peel an orange for herself.

'What does Ngaire have to say?'

'Oh, Ngaire.' I picked up an air-letter from my previous flat-mate in Wellington. It was the first she had written me. 'Oh, she thinks she's in love with someone down in Christchurch, only she didn't realize till he just got engaged to someone else,' I said rather flatly.

'Poor Ngaire. I expect she missed you when you went. She was never really one of the gang, was she?'

'Oh, not really. She thought they were crazy,' I added with sudden intuition.

'Yes, but you had such good times together,' my mother went on. 'I've still got some of your letters. I thought I might make a comedy play out of them one day, if you didn't object. Of course they'd have to be censored a bit.' She laughed, but when I turned to her I found she was looking at me curiously. 'You're a lot quieter now. Perhaps it's the lack of company. I think I'll get you some b.is.'

'Let's go down to the restaurant,' I said quickly, sliding off the bed into my boots. 'I could do with a huddle over the stove. I suppose Daddy's still talking to that man.'

The restaurant was long and clean and empty looking. The typical shiny black stove wound its way up into the ceiling. A group of thickly coated men were devouring mussels at one end of the room, and the irregular click of the shells divided the silence into pieces. We sat and sipped café russe, licking away the smooth cream from our lips. My father was busy talking to a man from the university, and soon we got into conversation with his long-faced daughter, who spoke halting English. Before she spoke she would look away hurriedly and mutter to herself, finding the right words.

During these intervals I found myself looking with furtive fascination at her very bad acne. It was not a common thing in Micald, in the same way that sickness was less common, with the exception of a mild form of diabetes. Therefore I couldn't help being slightly revolted. At the same time it touched a chord in my memory. Then I thought of Robert's photographs, and of the shadowy patches that could quite well have been acne. But surely—could I have been attracted by someone with pimples? Yet the more I thought about it, the nearer I seemed to be getting to Robert. Again it was smells which came to mind first—smells of tobacco and saliva. Then across my sight swam a picture of a frayed jersey, and of a figure sitting, with one knee raised, on an old colonial couch. I could see the face quite clearly now. It was strangely fixed, and there were tears upon it—large, wet tears. Before I had time to be astonished, I could see myself, in a green wool frock and flat, red earrings, toasting cheese on a crumbed and rusty oven tray. My hair had fallen over my forehead, and the thing I noticed mainly were my badly cared for hands and broken nails. Both these pictures were so clear that I remained staring into my glass cup when the girl had finished her careful speech. Then I blurted:

'Oh, yes, it must be very difficult,' hoping this was the right thing to say, and looked back at my nails. They were now well kept and varnished.

'Aren't you going to finish your drink, Di? What are you thinking of? I thought you'd be better company, I must say.'

10

THE next place I remember most clearly is Vienna. We arrived there late at night, and stacked our suitcases in the almost deserted station café. We had travelled at the last minute on a smaller train than usual, and hadn't been able to change money after crossing the border, as we'd expected to. We had had nothing to eat but a boiled egg each and a sip of camomile tea which a little German woman had offered us. Fortunately the change office had been open when our train came in. Now we bought rolls and sausages and warm, fluffy coffee, glancing at each other in grateful anticipation as we bore them to the table. The coffee tasted unexpectedly rubbery, but the sausages were strong and good, with blobs of creamy mustard.

'There'll be a load of mail at the hotel,' my mother said through greasy lips.

We had given our friends addresses and dates on which to write to us, where we had known them. It was nearly a fortnight now since we had had any mail. At the hotel a fat young man in a bright blue jersey led us up the bare corridor, past the bar door, which hummed with noise, and a broken cigarette machine, to our bedroom. He presented us with the door-key, attached to a big red rubber ball with a number on it, and backed his way out smiling. There were three beds with big, white soufflé eiderdowns and my mother sank on to the middle one, sending it puffing up on either side of her. I pounced on the pile of letters on the table and dealt them out like cards. There were three for me—from Robert, Stephen and Barry Morrison. I was laughing my way through Barry's harmless pornographies, when my mother said suddenly, disapprovingly:

'I don't know why you encourage Barry to write to you.'

'Why shouldn't I?' I asked with real curiosity.

'It isn't him particularly. It's just that I don't think it's quite fair to Robert—keeping up a correspondence with other boys.'

I was surprised. I had thought she held a secretly low opinion of Robert, but here she was defending him.

'Why, surely you don't object to Stephen?' I held up his unopened letter. 'He's just a friend of the family.'

'To stretch a point. I'd rather you wrote to Kathleen.'

'Oh, I have done. I think she prefers talking to writing.' I rolled over on to my back and tore Stephen's letter open with careful casualness. His writing was hurried and sprawled, but he wrote humorously and intelligently. The first page was a detailed account of his latest visit to the dentist, which had apparently been long overdue. I imagined him sitting stiffly in the dentist's chair, with the white bib clipped round his throat. The picture filled me with a pleasant feeling of intimacy. It was only next morning that I woke with a heavy throbbing in my lower jaw. I groaned, reaching for the mirror and examining my teeth.

'Trust Di to get toothache in a foreign country,' my mother frowned as I dressed with one hand to my face. 'And that wretched plug gurgled all night, keeping me awake. Oh, Gerald! These pipes are cold now! You just see, there won't be any water. There, it's icy. Where did you pack the burner?'

My father had risen and breakfasted earlier, as he intended to spend the day at the university, so my mother and I entered the restaurant together and headed for a table away from the smoke of the early customers' cigarettes.

'I know why the room was so cheap now,' my mother said, munching a roll and jam. 'They expect to make their money out of the food. We'll eat out after this. The coffee's good, anyway.'

'No, thank you. My tooth.' I looked round me drearily.

'Oh, Di. Is it really bad? Perhaps we could find a dentist. I'll ask the proprietor. Would you go to one?'

'Maybe he'll yank it out when it doesn't need it.'

'Well, make up your mind.'

'Oh, all right. I suppose I'll have to if I don't want it to spoil the whole trip. Bother Stephen writing about his dentist. I'm sure I would never have thought of having toothache otherwise,' I laughed.

I'll never forget my visit to 'Ludwig'—his second name didn't impress me and I've forgotten it. I had had little experience of real pain, in my very dull life, as I now judged it, and I was hardly prepared for the sharp spike of the drill. We found this dentist up a dusty, wooden staircase at one end of a shadowy corridor. The waiting-room was crowded with fat, apprehensive Austrians, but for some reason I was ushered ahead of them. Ludwig himself spoke no English, but a young man in the waiting-room was asked to stand by and translate my remarks. His English was fluid but garbled.

'I don't want it out,' I mouthed firmly and clearly at him and gripped the chair-arms as he translated.

Ludwig went about his job with earnest concentration and relentless brutality. His black brows lurched down over my frightened face, and withdrew as suddenly.

'The pain is less?' a voice said in my ear. I nodded, speechless with shock, and staggered up from the chair. My mother met me in the waiting-room, as I came out unsteadily in my clumsy boots.

'All right?'

'Dead,' I said thickly, and followed her down the stairs with my chin held stiffly at an angle. The hotel proprietor greeted us with a broad grin.

'All right? All right? A goot dentist, *hein*? A goot dentist?'

'Very good,' my mother spoke for me.

'And it's only temporary,' I groaned as we reached the bedroom.

'Did he say? Well, never mind, dear. Think of the concert tonight.'

'I think I'll write to Stephen and tell him off.'

'All right, dear, it's your affair.' She shrugged her fur coat on to the bed. She was wearing a red twin-set and I noticed how it suited her. I thought of my first experience of this colour and the sharp pain it had given me to look at it. Now it was a colour I was particularly fond of, although I had no clothes in it myself.

How grey Germany is!' my mother had said in Cologne. 'Perhaps it's the time of year.' I had agreed with her wholeheartedly, and yet it occurred to me soon after, that it was the type of dull greyness that I had been so well used to in Micald. My values must be changing already. The idea of this no longer filled me with panic. I was quite content to be influenced by this other self whose place I had taken over. I noted each change in myself with interest and even pleasure. By now I felt quite at home with my parents—a thing I would never have believed possible a few weeks back. Lying across the bed I pulled my writing-pad towards me and began on my letter to Stephen.

It had been arranged that I would accompany my parents as far as Syracuse, when they would continue on to Malta to pick up their boat on its way to New Zealand. And I would travel back to Paris by train, then catch the boat to England. I intended to find another job and stay in London for a further four or five months before I caught the boat, on which I had a berth, back to Wellington—and Robert. I told Stephen of my plans, hoping they would interest him.

I had discovered a lot of things from the weeks spent with my parents, and had the facts about myself ranged in much more order. This had given me greater confidence in myself and even room to relax a little. I think I behaved more naturally. My mother had expressed her pleasure at seeing me 'perking up', 'more myself'. As the ache in my jaw subsided, I found my painful visit to the dentist had left me strangely exhilarated. Somehow the experience had done me good. Its brutality had bared another of my senses, as my first glimpse of the red bus had done. I was beginning to think of my senses as covered by layer upon layer of protective bandage. Now I was discarding it, as apparently was necessary in this world. The idea excited me with its unknown quantities, and I rolled away from my letter restlessly.

'Weren't we going to the clock museum?' I asked. 'Let's go now, shall we? My tooth feels fine, and I'm hungry too.'

. . . . .

I left my parents at Syracuse as planned, and took the seven-fifteen morning train for Rome. The carriage was empty to begin with, and I spread my things about me on the seat—my *Saturday Evening Post* and sunglasses, my camera in its canvas case. This case had been bought separately and was far too large for the camera. Down the side I had crammed two hard-boiled eggs and a bread roll for my lunch.

In Italy I had my first experience of spring in this new world. We had travelled into the hotter weather almost overnight, and it had taken me by surprise as much as the cold had done in London. It was several degrees warmer than I had ever known our hot season to be in Micald, and the coolest clothes I had in my suitcase were a blouse and skirt which I wore now. At this time it was early April, and I had learnt that it would be spring in England, though cooler than Italy. I was looking forward to this.

In fact there were a lot of things to look forward to, quite suddenly. Stephen had written telling me he had arranged to spend Easter in Paris, and as I would be arriving there at about the same time, suggested I stay on a few days and enjoy the sights with him.

'Don't expect that I'll show you a wild night life,' he wrote. 'It'll be my first time in Paris, and also I'm not very rich at present.'

Nevertheless, my imagination flew ahead of me in anticipating these few days. During our trip I had tired of watching the scenery from the train, and joined my father in reading paper-backed novels. I thought of the Paris of Somerset Maugham and my toes curled with excitement. With my parents I had stayed only one night in Paris, before leaving next morning for Louvain. As we were leaving my father had booked a room for me, for the night I intended to stay there on my way back to England. I wrote to tell Stephen of this, and wasn't long in getting his reply.

I've managed to book a room at the same hotel, and I've told them you'll need your room till the end of the week.

So it was all settled. I didn't tell my parents of my changed plans, and hoped that my impatience with the rest of our holiday wasn't too apparent. The carriage soon filled at Taormina, and I confined myself to my window seat. The warm, foreign voices splashed over me, and I felt a mood of recklessness come upon me. A dark, Italian-looking boy, with very bright eyes and teeth, kept turning these upon me with an engaging grin, and I took up my magazine quickly. His eye fell on it.

'Oh, you're English?'

I nodded, stiffening.

'But I speak a little English. I lived there for a little time. It is a good country England. You like Italy?'

'Yes—well, I haven't been here long.'

'It's not my country, you know. My country is Rumania.'

He began to tell me about this place where he was born.

'So you are English?' he went on suddenly. 'Yes, when I was in England there was a girl I knew very well. We lived together a long time. It was only a few months ago, then I came over here.'

Fascinated, I waited for him to go on talking. He did so.

'My English girl, she was not really beautiful, you know—

but she had a wonderful heart. Being with her was like being married. Nothing but just to save the money, you know, and be happy together. You don't know what that girl was capable of. Unselfish!'

'She must have loved you,' said rather hoarsely.

'I think, yes, she is suffering, you know. When you have been with a person that way, you remember. She will forget me, you know, if she lives with another man, but not for a while I think.'

'She might always remember you,' I surprised myself by saying. In fact the whole conversation surprised me, to put it mildly. After all, here we had only met a few minutes ago, and now this young man——

'Oh, no. I don't think she'll always remember me,' he laughed. After a pause he went on: 'You are a good girl. I can see you are a good girl.'

I looked bewildered and he said quickly, teasingly: 'Perhaps you don't like that. But what I mean is, some girls, and English girls too, they lead a man on and then—no! If a girl is like that, you know, I am mad. I beat her—I don't care—as if she were a man. Hurt her. But if she is honest with me I am good with her. There was a Polish girl, you know, who was like that—rotten, but lovely, lovely. I thought I'd get her one day, acting the Spaniard. Make myself speak the broken English, you know—"Plenty cigarettes, Americano." And she was a bit drunk, you know—didn't realize. And when I got her home I lock the door. Click! No escape, then we make love a little, and when I'm getting to the point— No. She jump like that. But by now I know she is no angel, so I beat her—this way, that! And she saying "Santa Maria, Santa Maria!" Catholic you know. And I say to her: "Don't bring the name of a saint into this situation—because you are a steencker! And soon she say, would I let her go if she let me have what I wanted. So I say, of course—though by now I hate her, but I never refuse a girl if she wants me. But I am like a dog with her, you know. Just as she starts to get the pleasure—finish! Like that. Oh, she was mad! Cursing at me in Polish—and I understand of course. I know the Slavic languages, you know. And I laughed! She was mad, you know. Mad!'

We had stopped and he jumped to the window to buy a bottle of cheap wine from a passing refreshment-wagon. I watched it wobble in the little round bottle as the train drew out. I felt shaken by the torrent of words and heard myself give a gasp for breath. It was as if I had been mentally bruised and slapped into a new awareness.

'You like some?'

'Just a little, thank you.'

He left the train before Rome, and I was left to my *Saturday Evening Post*. However, it wouldn't be long before the train would arrive. I had a room booked in a hotel at Rome, so as to avoid having to sleep on trains. I thought of running to catch a bus from the station, in the dark, and felt suddenly frightened. Of course, I could get a taxi. . . . Then I had an idea. Suppose I went straight on to Milan, and then to Paris? Stephen was arriving a day before I was due, so he would be there already. Impatience to see him urged me to do so. Surely I could get a room somewhere, if not at the same hotel? A porter at Rome directed me to the Milan train which was just leaving.

'*Corrente, corrente*,' he shouted. And I ran, with my suitcase bumping against my legs.

The train was full of soldiers going home for Easter. Several of them tried to 'make a pass' at me, so I spent the night on a small seat outside the ladies' toilet, where I felt safer. My experience was widening quite suddenly.

I left the train at Milan, feeling curiously light-headed, and realized that I'd eaten nothing but one egg since Syracuse. After finding what time the Paris train left, I checked in my luggage, and went out to find a *trattoria*. Here I had a meal of spaghetti and my remaining boiled egg. I still had quite an amount of Italian money left, which I had intended to spend in Rome. In the same mood of recklessness I walked in the hot city sun and bought a rather unusual summer frock, catching my train at the very last minute. I noticed my finger-nail had broken.

II

THE hotel was in the Rue Molière, a small street not far from the Louvre. I arrived there at ten o'clock in the morning and was relieved to find my room would be available right away. I followed Madame's fat son up the winding stairway with my cases. My room was a tiny attic one, with dark red sacking curtains and bedspread. Another piece of sacking hung along the wall at the side of the bed. I peered behind it suspiciously after dropping my cases, and was relieved to see only a rather dirty stretch of wallpaper.

Sitting down on the bed I gave a sigh of fatigue and contentment. I looked around me and wondered what Stephen's room was like. This one was the cheapest in the hotel, so his would no doubt be a little more luxurious. What could I do till he arrived—which would be about lunch-time? I began to unpack a few things, and came across my writing-case. Bother, I should write to Robert. Throwing it on the bed, I washed off the dust of travel, tried on my new frock, then took it off again. Lying on the bed in my slip, I took up my writing-pad.

Darling Robert [I began],

  Something awful is happening. I think I'm falling out of love with you. Perhaps it should end here. Don't think I'll ever, ever forget——

Oh damn. It was no use trying to write in his own style. I couldn't take it seriously. Tearing the page off I threw it into the tin rubbish-bin. I had been certain for some days now. I could never marry him. I had woken up one night in Venice, from a dream in which he figured. It had left me feeling as if I knew him quite well. He was no longer just a photograph and a pile of letters. Thinking of him reminded me, quite clearly now, of long, complicated conversations, sitting somewhere in the cold dark, all the time longing to creep into bed and close my pricking eyes. Why hadn't I? What was it that had kept me from saying good night? What had I been waiting for? What was I trying to discover from these long, circuitous dualogues. All that remained with me now was the feel of my bare feet in flat suède shoes, my stinging eyelids, and the devouring tiredness. I gave up trying to write and looked at my watch. Good heavens! One o'clock already! I slid quickly into my new frock, pulling the collar into an elegant position, and went to the door. I was halfway down the twisty stairs when I heard Stephen talking to Madame. I met him coming up. He stared at me.

'You here already?'

'Uhuh. I decided not to spend the night in Rome.' A silly smile kept taking hold of my lips.

'You can stay here tonight then?'

'Yes, my room was free, luckily.'

'That's all right then.' He smiled. 'That's very all right. Where's your room, anyway?'

I pointed up the twisted staircase. 'Right at the top.'

He gave an amused frown. 'Oh dear. I'm right here.' He took out the key. 'Come on in and help me unpack. You weren't going anywhere, were you?'

'No, of course not. I'm a bit hungry though. How about lunch?'

'Haven't you had it? I have, I'm sorry. Still, we'll buy you a yard or two of bread. What would you like with it—cheese? Sausage? I'll get it for you. Have a map.' He pointed to a pile of travel pamphlets on the dresser and made for the door. When he had gone I picked up a map of Paris and tried to focus my eyes on it. I found a small pulse beating in my temple prevented me from doing so, and gave up trying just as Stephen returned.

'Marvellous stuff,' he said, biting the end off the loaf and putting his feet up on the bed. I cut a couple of slices with his pocket-knife, and sandwiched the sausage. 'What's the matter? Sit down. You know, I'd forgotten how quiet you were. You were much more talkative in your letters.'

'Yes, that's a lot easier.'

'I'm sure you've got a lot to talk about. What is it scares you?'

'Nothing scares me. I'll talk soon, I expect. I just take a long time warming up.' I blushed.

'Well, don't forget. I'm really quite a good listener too, although I talk so much.'

'Yes.'

'You believe me? Well, that's something. Do you mind if I eat some more of your bread?' He bounced up. He seemed to be in a much gayer mood than I had ever known him. Perhaps making up for my own shyness? I made an effort.

'What were you going to do today?'

'Nothing much—wait for you. What do you feel like doing? How about exploring Montmartre?'

'Sounds lovely. All of Paris sounds lovely.' My voice seemed to spill out, and Stephen looked up at me.

'I hope you'll think so at the end of the week.'

Coming back, tired from our long walk, we noticed a dimly lit restaurant which looked attractively romantic through the pale gold windows.

'Not too dear.' Stephen studied the menu at the door. 'And there's a negress singing at eight. Shall we try it?'

'Oh, yes, please. Let's go back first though. I want to change.'

The negress didn't sing. We waited for her through mushroom omelette, ice-cream and coffee, which we dragged out for as long as possible. At last we left reluctantly. The meal had cost us about a pound each, with tips.

'Well, we won't eat there again.' Stephen took my arm. 'I'm awfully sorry. It wasn't much good, was it?'

'The plates were nice, anyway.'

'Should have pocketed one.' He steered me fiercely through the hotel doorway, and didn't drop my arm until outside his door. 'What on earth'll we do? It's only nine o'clock. We should have bought a paper to see what's going on. Come in, anyway. You don't think you shouldn't, do you?'

'No, of course not. Do I look like a prude?' A quiver went through me to hear myself talk like this.

'No. But I think you are one.' He took off his coat and sprawled on the bed among his pamphlets of Paris. 'Come on up and help me make plans for tomorrow.' He looked at me challengingly, and I sat gingerly on the bedspread. 'Are you interested in museums and things?' he asked.

'Not terribly. We visited so many in the last two months.'

'Of course you did. I forgot. Will your parents be on the boat now?' he asked.

'No, tomorrow.'

'I hope you don't wish you were going with them?'

'I don't,' I muttered with a vehemence that surprised me.

'Not pining to get home?'

'No.'

'What about Robert?'

'What about him?'

'I mean, don't you want to get back to him?'

'I suppose so. But you see, I've been remembering things' —I blushed—'things about him that I don't like. They didn't seem to matter before—but now they do.'

'I don't suppose they'll matter when you see him again.'

I didn't reply, but looked down at a photo of the Eiffel Tower.

'What made you give up the night you intended to spend in Rome, anyway?' Stephen picked up the photo as if to see what there was in it that interested me.

'Oh,' I shrugged. 'It was dark. I think I was afraid of being picked up by someone before I got to my hotel. It didn't make much difference, anyway, 'cos the train to Milan was full of soldiers——'

'Getting amorous?' Stephen suggested.

'Not really amorous. They were just animals.'

Stephen gave a burst of laughter. 'You're a funny girl. You must have been travelling a long time. Two nights, was it?'

'And three days.'

'Diana.'

I looked up startled to see his head quite close to mine.

'Isn't it funny, that's the first time I've kissed you?' he sighed.

'Not funny.' My voice trembled a little.

'I usually get around to it much sooner. Oh, Di, why did you come here?'

'I had to, on my way back to England, silly.'

'But why did you stay?'

'Because you were here, and you told me to.'

'You knew it would be like this, didn't you?'

'I suppose so.'

'I meant it to be. Because you're so sweet. Oh, Di, this is awful.'

I sat up. 'What's awful?'

'Oh, God.'

I watched him striding round the room, sitting with my lips still parted. I thought he must be acting. A few minutes ago he had been quite sensible, and now all this. 'What's awful?' I repeated.

'Oh, it's not awful for you.' He turned round quickly.

'No.' On the contrary, I was warm with an extraordinary new happiness. He stared at me.

'I can't make you out. I wish to God you'd talk. If I only knew——' He strode across and put his hands on my shoulders. 'You know what I want to find out.'

I shook my head slowly. Several possibilities occurred to me—he wanted to know if I'd agree to making love—if I was still in love with Robert. 'Ask me,' I said desperately.

'Can't,' he said after a pause. 'Oh, Di,' he moved his arms round me, 'please.'

'Stephen——' I began, then broke off. 'Oh, I feel so queer. I'm going up to bed.'

'Oh, God, I thought you were going to talk at last.' He stood up suddenly. 'You're not going to be ill, are you?'

'No, I don't think so.' I smiled at him. He took my arm and escorted me absent-mindedly to my door.

12

AFTER this we began to treat each other, quite suddenly, with more familiarity. Yesterday had been Monday and the shops had been shut. Now they were open and I insisted on visiting some of the larger dress shops. Stephen was in a bad mood, and kept suggesting cups of coffee which he drank while scowling slightly. After lunch we visited Notre Dame Cathedral and the Latin Quarter.

'It would be marvellous to live here, for a while, wouldn't it?' He brightened and quickened his step. 'Wait a minute. That bookshop.'

I hurried to keep up with him as he jerked me across the road.

'Blast this silly traffic! If it would only go the right way.'

'What amazes me,' he said later, 'are all these little toddlers speaking perfect French. When I think of how long it took me——!'

'Oh, Stephen, you are silly!' I laughed to see his low spirits deserting him.

By the time we reached the hotel, however, we were silent and grumpy with fatigue. Stephen had bought more bread and sausage to save money, and we ate it in his room.

'We should be having a good meal of meat and vegetables,' I reproached him. 'I'm not broke yet, you know.'

'Don't you like this stuff? I could eat it for ever.' He snapped the bread in half.

'Yes, and a lot of good it would do you.'

'Oh, you don't worry about that, surely?'

When we had cleared away the meal, Stephen plugged in his electric razor, so I began to repair my nails.

'Do you have to do your nails with that stuff?' He turned round irritably. 'It stinks. Pouf! Horrible!'

I screwed the cap on the bottle, 'I'll do it upstairs if you like,' and walked out stiffly.

'No, wait, Di. I just——' His voice stopped as I rounded the first turn in the stair. It was dark and I had difficulty finding the keyhole. There was no light in the passage. In my room I uncapped the bottle and finished my nails with a few flicks of the brush. The red sacking moved at the window, and I rose to shut out the wind. Then I changed my mind and flapped my hands out of the window to dry the nails. It was quite chilly outside by now, and the lights of the street seemed a long way down. I drew my hands in, and went to sit on the bed, frowning. There was a tap on the door and Stephen came in with a folded newspaper. He stopped.

'What an odd little room. Suits you.'

'What did you want?'

He crossed and took up my hands. 'Not wet?' He kissed them. 'I'm sorry, Di. I don't know what's the matter with me. You must think I'm awful. I am awful.'

'Oh, no.' I smiled.

'I am. I wish you knew me better. I feel as if I've known you such a long time. I suppose I have, technically. Since you were six and a half.'

'No, you haven't,' I burst out suddenly.

'What do you mean?'

A feeling of uneasiness came over me. 'I keep thinking you're imagining I'm someone else. All the time you're—kissing me—like this.'

'But—who on earth?'

'Oh, I don't know. It's just a feeling.'

'Di, I'm only thinking of you. There's no one else I'd think of. You don't like being synthetic?' he added.

'No,' I said firmly.

'Well, neither do I. You don't confuse me with Robert when you shut those eyes?'

'I don't like Robert.' I bent my head quickly, away from his face.

'What?'

'I've been trying to tell him.'

'But that's it!' He looked incredulous.

'That's what?'

'What I wanted you to tell me.' He lifted my ringed finger and let it fall. 'Oh, Di, I'm so happy.' He pressed close to me and ran his fingers through my hair. 'Diana.' His voice sounded to be coming from a long way off. 'I want to be an animal!' He said this with a note of laughter, then—'Oh, darling, darling, help me not to.' His body seemed to strain, then relaxed suddenly.

'You're looking so frightened.' He stroked my arm. I was trembling quite violently. 'Mustn't frighten you.' His own heart was beating noisily into mine. 'You wouldn't be an animal, not even in a cold way, would you?'

'No, I wouldn't. I wouldn't dare.'

He laughed and said: 'Oh, darling, I think you're lovely. You're a very, very little girl,' and fell asleep.

I listened to his heavy breathing in surprise. My own was quick and frightened. Gradually it subsided, and I lay in a curious state of peace. I looked at the veins across his eyelids. He had been so theatrical. I almost couldn't believe it had happened. And yet it was so nice, lying here, with him. It was warm and reassuring. I thought of how cold the room had seemed when I was in it alone. The folded newspaper lay at the back of Stephen's head, and I leant across to take it. He sat up.

'Uh, sorry.' He grinned at me sleepily, then bent and kissed my ear before standing up. 'Yes, we're going out.' He indicated the newspaper.

'Where to? It's nearly half past eight.'

'It doesn't start till nine or something. Comédie Française. *L'annonce Faite à Marie*. Do you want to?'

'Good idea. Go away then and let me change. You've crushed me to bits.'

I understood very little of the play. It was extremely hot in the theatre, and grew hotter as the play progressed. We spent most of the first interval running down the many stairs for bottles of Coke, which were warm and frothy, to our disappointment. The performance finished very late and we arrived home absent-minded with weariness.

Stephen slept late next morning, but at seven I found myself impatiently wide awake. I lingered over dressing and went downstairs to peep round Stephen's door. He was lying on his stomach, with his clothes on his feet. His trousers had slid off into a heap on the floor, so I crept in and folded them. I sat at his dressing-table for half an hour, reading a copy of *Vile Bodies*, which he had left lying there, face up. When he still didn't wake I wrote him a note, and went out for a walk.

The weather had unexpectedly turned cold, and there was a fierce wind blowing, so I had put on my coat and boots. Swinging along towards the Louvre I felt contented and sure of myself. I crossed the Pont Neuf and continued along beside the river, counting the bridges off on my map, and lingering at the bookstalls to finger the grubby volumes. At the Eiffel Tower I crossed and paused to work out my way to the Étoile. Walking up the Champs Élysées I noticed with pleasure that the sidewalk cafés were open and doing business. In the Tuileries children were playing noisily and bowling hoops among the trees. I bought coffee and a handful of liquorice sweets at a busy little kiosk. It was moving round to midday by this time. I had walked farther then I'd intended. Outside the Louvre I broke into a trot. It was warmer now, but the wind was still quite cool, and I noticed my boots had been chafing at my ankles, leaving them red and raw.

'You might have waited for me.' Stephen met me at the bottom of the stairs. He turned to go back up.

'I went too far,' I explained breathlessly. 'Then I had to come back.'

'Why not get a bus, or something?'

'I would have got the wrong one. Oh, Stephen, my ankles are sore as anything.'

'You're a silly,' he said, as I pulled off my boots in his room. 'Have you got any vaseline or anything?'

'Yes, on the top of my dressing-table. Would you like to get it, please?'

We stayed home for the rest of the afternoon. Stephen tried to solve a French crossword puzzle, while I read his book, *Vile Bodies*. We were both comfortably tired and smiled across at each other at contented intervals.

. . . . .

It was two nights later that I woke to find Stephen standing at the side of my bed. I managed to control a start and said, without lifting my head:

'What's the matter?'

'I wanted to tell you something.'

'What is it?' I sat up and lifted my watch from the dresser.

'Ten past twelve,' he said quickly. 'Can I come in there with you?'

I laughed at him.

'No, but it's so damn cold out here,' he persisted.

I looked at his bare feet. 'Well, why not tell me quickly, then?'

'It might take a long time.'

'Oh, all right.' I turned down the covers and shuffled over against the wall. He followed and put his arm around me.

'I love you.'

I was silent, then a laugh fluttered in my chest and flew out.

'What's funny?'

'Nothing. You said it might take a long time.'

'It could.'

'What do you mean?'

He lifted his body on one elbow and looked down at me.

'Stephen, go away, you're frightening me.'

'Is that all?' He dropped back on to his shoulder.

'No. I mean, I don't understand. You've mixed me up.' I was afraid he would go away.

'Well, just lie there a minute and get unmixed. I'll wait for you.'

We both lay silently for a while, then he said hurriedly:

'Don't go to sleep.'

'I couldn't if I tried.' I smiled in the darkness.

'You're the most tantalizing female. I don't think you do it on purpose either. How did you feel when I said that, just now—about loving you?'

'Why should I tell you?'

'It's me that loves you. You want someone to love you, don't you? I thought you wanted it an awful lot.'

'Doesn't everyone?'

'I suppose so, but you keep pretending not to.' He stopped talking and began to kiss me again. I felt his hand at my pyjama buttons. Moving away, I said jerkily:

'Go on talking, Stephen.'

'Why?'

'I'm frightened.'

'Oh, Di, darling, I love you. Don't you understand? I love you. Let me make you happy.'

'Of course I understand. I'm just frightened.'

'Is that all? Nothing else?'

So we made love, and the wind made noises behind the red sacking.

We woke with the sun on our faces. Stephen smiled across at me and said in a low voice:

'I made love to you.'

'Yes.'

'Happy?'

'Oh, yes.'

'You're mine, now, aren't you?'

'Was I very difficult?' I asked with curiosity.

'Not at all.' His face clouded suddenly.

'I suppose you've done it before,' I hurried to say.

'Kind of.'

'How, kind of?'

'Never like this. Because I love you.' His face clouded again. 'With Robert, did you——?'

'No, never. Not with anyone.' I almost added: 'I'm sure of it'—because I was.

'Oh, darling, of course you didn't. You're lovely, lovely. You used to give me electric shocks when I touched you.'

'Don't I now?' I laughed at him.

'Yes, but not nearly so painful.'

'Good heavens, we don't want the maid to find us here.' I clasped my watch around my wrist. 'How are you going to get downstairs?'

'Run like the devil.' He fastened up his pyjama jacket and made for the door.

'Don't go down a flight too many and land in the dining-room.'

'That reminds me.' He put his head back in. 'We'll have a whopping breakfast out, shall we? No bread and cheese today.'

'Definitely, no.' I listened to his bare feet receding.

'Let's go back to the hotel,' Stephen said as we left the café, later.

'Why?'

'There's nothing to do. I'd rather talk.'

'Me, too. But what about?'

'About you not going back to New Zealand.'

'Aren't I?'

'Not in four months.'

'Oh.'

'Why? You don't want to?' he asked, as we reached his room.

'Of course not.'

'What do you want to do?' he grinned, pulling me to sit on the bed with him.

'Well, I'll get a job and stay in England, I suppose.'

'You're not getting another live-in job,' he said.

'Oh, why not? That's what I planned on.'

'I want you to live with me.'

I stared at him. 'How do you mean?'

'Well, we could get married.' He looked towards me quickly. 'What do you think of the idea?'

'No, I couldn't do that.'

'No?' He gave an embarrassed laugh. 'What's wrong? I mean—don't you want to?'

'You'd soon stop loving me. You don't know me very well. You'd get to know things about me—and wish you hadn't—married me, I mean.'

'What could I get to know?'

'There, you see, you're worried already.'

'I'm not.' He looked angry, then softened and leant towards me. 'I'm quite sure, Di—I'll never want to leave you. But you just don't want to marry me, is that it?'

'Not marry.' I looked frightened. 'Don't get angry, Stephen.'

'All right.' He kissed me. 'It was wonderful last night, wasn't it?'

I nodded.

'You're quite sure?'

'Of course.'

'Then let's work something out. We could get somewhere to live—together—just pretend we were married. For a year or so. Try it out.' He was speaking jerkily and frowning.

'Yes, I'd like that.'

'Oh, darling. I'd look after you—make sure you didn't have a baby. We'd be happy, wouldn't we?'

'Oh, yes.' I raised my head. 'Stephen.'

'Mmm?'

'Could I be having one now?'

'You mean last night?'

'Yes.'

'Of course you could. Good heavens, you should know.

'Yes. I just hadn't thought of it.'

'Would it be terrible?'

'I'd have to marry you, wouldn't I?'

'That's right.' He grinned. 'Don't worry about it. Everything's so marvellous, now. When I think—in a couple of days it's back to those wretched Standard Twos.'

'Oh, I just thought. What will Maureen say?' I flushed at the memory of her prim bearing.

'Oh, don't mind Maureen. I've shocked her before, and she's harder than she looks. Kathleen, now, *she'll* be delighted!'

13

WE RETURNED to London two days later. I had originally intended to stay at the Feathers until I found myself a job. My father had provided me with enough money to last the two or three weeks until this time. Now, however, I found I had spent nearly half this money in Paris, and on my new frock. It was more urgent than ever that I should waste no time in finding a job. Stephen said he knew of a place in Reigate where we could almost certainly get rooms. Meanwhile, I checked in at the Feathers and Stephen returned to his school at Salfords, half a day late.

'What about nursing?' Stephen had suggested when I told him I couldn't type. 'Oh, no, it's not very good pay. Psychiatric though—they pay better.'

'That's an idea. It would be interesting, wouldn't it? I don't want anything dull.'

'Oh, it would be that all right. But hard work.'

So I wrote to the matron at Selwyn Hospital and made an appointment for an interview. It was agreed that I start work on the following Monday. I met Stephen for dinner to tell him about it.

'Now shut up a minute and let me tell you *my* news.' He speared a piece of curried rabbit.

'Yes?' I looked up at him.

'We move into our new home tomorrow,' he grinned.

'What's it like?'

'Only one room, I'm afraid—but absolutely huge. And there's a little alcove with stove and sink, etcetera. We'll have to share a bathroom. Does that matter?'

'Not really. How much, anyway?'

'Two ten, and pennies in the gas.'

'Have you told Maureen?'

'Yes,' he laughed at me.

'What did she say?'

'She wasn't very surprised.'

'But what did she say?'

'Look, stop worrying about what people think.' He paused. 'She's lending us some bedclothes and crockery. And I think she said an iron. The furniture's pretty dreadful, but there's a lovely big bed.'

The following day I spent filling the cupboards and drawers from our suitcases, and rearranging the furniture. Stephen arrived early in the evening, and we opened a tin of mulligatawny soup.

'The woman upstairs came and introduced herself,' I told him, picking up the hot soup dish.

'Oh, lord, no.' Stephen raised his head. 'I hope you didn't forget that you were Mrs Bartlett.'

'No, I didn't. It sounded so funny though. I didn't ask her in because of the mess, but she kept peering round the door.'

'Perhaps you should have done. But no, we don't want to get too friendly with people. They get too inquisitive.'

'Isn't it a bit sordid?'

'Only if you think it is. I think it's fun. Don't be silly, of course it's not sordid,' he added, as I still looked doubtful.

'Well, then, I wish it wasn't so complicated—having my mail sent to the hospital instead of here. What will Mummy think?'

'She'll think you live in, like most of the nurses do.'

'And supposing she asks?'

'You can skirt around it. Anyway—one little lie—I've decided you've too much of a conscience. You'd be a lot happier without.' He pushed his plate back.

'But, Stephen?'

'Yes?'

'You've got a conscience with me, haven't you? I mean—you wouldn't tell me a lie or anything?'

'Darling.' He pulled me on to his knee.

'Mind my spoon.'

'Darling,' he went on, 'I love you, I'd never lie to you. We've got to trust each other completely, haven't we?'

'Yes.'

'Well, what's the matter?'

'I feel silly with the light on.'

'Oh, all right.' He bounced his knees and let me slide to the floor. 'What did you mean, anyway?' after a pause. 'The light was on in Paris. Did you feel silly then?'

'Sort of. What's the matter?' He was looking at me, frowning, and didn't shift his gaze for some seconds. Then he said:

'I'll turn it off then. We'll do the dishes later.' He moved towards me in the dark. 'Honeymoons are always hell. You'll get over it.'

'Are they? Have you done this before?'

'Supposing I said yes?' His voice sounded almost pleased by my question, and his teeth flashed white in the dark.

'But—you can't have done—can you?'

'I did try it once before. That time it *was* sordid. We lived in London—actually it was her flat. But don't worry, I didn't love her. It was just a mistake. I've never loved anyone till you. Well, go on, say something.'

'What about?'

'Don't you want to know anything about her?'

'Not particularly.' I remember how taut I was holding my body. There was a silence, then Stephen went on talking, rather defiantly.

'She was a bitch, anyway, and she had pimples on her back. She had a funny way of walking though—rather cute. She wasn't fat, but her arms and legs were rather plump. I remember once I said she had round wrists, and she almost threw a fit. I told her her eyes were round, too. She didn't like the word "round" at all.' He kept pausing between sentences, to see if I would say anything. 'You don't think I talk too much?'

'It doesn't matter.'

'She was very difficult to seduce. I didn't think she was scared—just hard-hearted. One day we were reading Van de Velde, lying on her bed together, and suddenly it was quite easy. I don't know what happened. She seemed quite pleased with herself afterwards—never stopped talking about it. In fact she got rather low-minded. She had a very peculiar private vocab. You don't mind me talking about this?'

'It doesn't matter.'

'You said that before.'

'Oh, sorry.'

'You see, I want to tell you everything now. We shouldn't have any secrets. I want you to tell me everything, too. You're not annoyed about anything, are you?'

'No, it isn't that. I'm just not very interested.'

'Well, you must be queer then.' He sounded suddenly childish.

'Yes, I think I am. I told you you wouldn't like me, as you discovered things about me.'

'I never said I didn't like you. I love you. I want to know everything about you.'

'What sort of things?'

'Well—if you ever did anything awful, that you've stored up without telling anyone.'

'What a morbid mind you've got. What makes you think I've done something like that?'

'Nothing. Only I've done plenty, and I hoped you had, too.'

'Well, I can't think of anything offhand. Can you wait a while?'

'In that case—how many men have there been in your life?'

'Oh, Stephen, you are nosy.'

'I explained——'

'All right, all right. Now let's see. There was Barry—and Robert, of course.'

'Of course. Who was Barry?'

'Just a boy.'

'Was he in love with you?'

'I don't know.' I said it impatiently.

'Well, what did you do with him? Where did you go?'

'Oh, pictures and things.'

'Dances?'

'I suppose so.'

'What did he look like?'

'Is that important?'

'Well, did you ever want to go to bed with him?'

'No, I didn't. And that's all I'm saying about Barry. You can read his next letter when I get it.'

'Letter? Does he write to you?' He sounded horrified.

'Now and then. A lot of rubbish.'

'Well, you're not writing to him. Have you got any letters from him that I could read now?'

'Sit down. I threw them out when I unpacked.'

'You sure?'

'Of course I'm sure. *I* don't tell lies.'

'Neither do I. Diana, please, don't quarrel. Come and kiss me.' He lay back on the bed and drew me down to him. 'Now tell me about the others,' he said a few minutes later.

'The other what?'

'Men in your life.' He said it almost timidly.

'Oh, for heaven's sake!'

He started as I jerked away. 'All right, don't jump out of your skin. I only wanted to know. There must have been others.'

'Oh, I expect so.'

'You expect? Don't you know?'

'Of course. But there's nobody important enough to remember. I don't keep asking you about your girl friends,' I added.

'No. I wish you would.' He paused. 'Did Kathleen tell you anything about my girl friends?'

'Not much.'

'Oh, what did she say?'

'I told you—nothing much. I don't remember. Something about a girl upsetting your 'varsity exams.'

'Oh, that's Linda. What did she say about her?'

'Nothing at all.' I shut my mouth tight.

'She was a funny girl. As tall as me, and terribly, terribly pale. She was short-sighted too, but she wouldn't wear glasses. It wouldn't have mattered.' He waited a moment then went on. 'She was awfully neurotic. I used to think I was madly in love with her.' He was silent for so long this time that I said:

'Weren't you?'

'No, she was a nymphomaniac.'

'You mean to say you didn't like it?'

'Sometimes. But she scared me. She was quite crazy at times. The things she said . . . She had a funny smell, too.'

'How do you mean?'

'I mean she had a funny smell. She wouldn't use perfume. Oh, she was clean. She just had a smell.'

I couldn't help laughing. 'I hope I haven't.'

'Why? I didn't mind it. Rather attractive.'

The next day was Saturday and Stephen lay in bed till nearly midday. I left him there, reading the paper, and took some washing to the laundrette just around the corner. Watching the clothes turn over and over in the suds, I tried to marshal my thoughts. Two things were uppermost in my mind—one of them my coming job in the mental hospital, the other Stephen. At the same time as feeling unusually happy and reassured by his company, I was wondering how long I would continue to keep it. I was afraid I might start needing him in the way he seemed to need me. Even now, the thought of his tiring of me made me feel limp and miserable. I watched my neighbour spread her clothes in the dryer, and followed her movements mechanically. Already I was finding it a strain keeping up the pretence that I was the same Diana Clouston who had lived in this world for nineteen years. Now I had to add to this the pretence that I was Mrs Bartlett. I felt as if my mind was full of bulging cupboards whose doors kept threatening to burst open. All the same, Stephen loved me. It was a nice feeling. Outside, a fat, blind woman walked slowly along the gutter singing 'Santa Lucia' in a thin, high voice and holding a shabby black handbag in front of her stomach. I was watching her through the glass windows when a voice said at my elbow: 'Hallo, I'm up.'

'Yes, I can see that.' It was Stephen, unshaven and smiling.

'Let's buy something mad for lunch. The woman upstairs is having kippers. Nearly stunk the place out. I'm starving.'

.   .   .   .   .

The next evening he snatched the paper out of my hands as I sat reading it, and said explosively: 'You're driving me mad!'

'What's the matter?'

'I'm going crazy!'

I laughed at him. 'Well, I can't help it.'

'Yes, you can. Stop reading and talk to me.'

'All right.'

'No, not like that. Look as if you want to. Don't you want to?'

'Yes, of course, Stephen. I'm just mystified.'

'Oh, don't keep calling me Stephen.' He lit a cigarette viciously.

'Well, that's your name, isn't it? Would you prefer Steve?'

'No, I wouldn't. Can't you think of anything else?'

'What like?'

'Like.... What do I call you?'

'Oh.' He wanted me to call him darling. I suppressed a laugh. He looked at me suspiciously.

'You never will, will you?'

'It's a bit difficult. Don't rush me.'

'What's difficult about it. What did you call Robert?'

'I'd known Robert longer.'

'I suppose you think I'm silly.'

'No, of course I don't,' I told him.

'It's just . . . I feel this affair's lopsided.'

'I'm sorry. I suppose it is. I don't mean to be like this. I just am. And I'm trying not to be.' I said this with sudden sincerity.

'Perhaps, if you didn't try too hard . . .'

'Don't let's talk about it then.' I went to the table and picked up the nylon nightdress which lay there folded. I stroked it.

'Do you like it?' Stephen looked pleased.

'Like it? I chose it, didn't I? It's lovely. Even if I freeze.'

'I'll make sure you're warm. Darling Di, I love you when you smile. I love you all the time. I love you. Please come to bed.'

14

I PRESENTED myself at the hospital on the following Monday. It was a loosely rambling, red-brick building placed high in the Surrey hills. To reach it, one had either to take the private coach which followed a narrow zigzag road through a tunnel of trees, or walk up a series of shallow steps across the fields. The coach had already left at the time I arrived at the foot of the hill, so I began the monotonous climb.

The moment I entered the big main doors and passed the enquiry desk, the hospital atmosphere struck me—the smell of disinfectant and the hurrying of nurses' footsteps in a distant corridor. The walls were hung with huge prints of modern paintings, and, oddly, their bright luridness served more than anything to remind me that I was in a mental hospital. The matron was coming out of her office as I approached, followed by a large Collie dog. She greeted me absently, and took me to be fitted out with a uniform. The sewing-room was warm and whirring with little black machines. A fat woman in a white overall led me into a back room and turned me round thoughtfully.

'You'll have to get some black stockings, luv. Here, let me show you how to fix your cap—have you got any pins?' She raised her warm-smelling arms to my head. 'Now a coat. We're a bit short on coats.' She rattled through the hangers. 'This here's about the nearest we've got. It'll do, won't it?'

I looked at myself in the mirror. The thick, black ARP coat hung heavily on my shoulders and stopped short several inches above the striped uniform.

'Keep you warm, anyway. When are you on?'

'Now, I think.'

'Well, you'd better leave the rest of these to be named. Have you got a laundry bag? I'll have one for you when you come back. You'd better hop along to Assistant now. Do you know how to get there?'

I went where she directed and soon I was following a sister and a newly engaged orderly along the bare corridor. The orderly was small and timid and I wondered if I looked as apprehensive as she did. To reach Ward One we had to pass through the adjoining sitting-room. The patients were distributed tidily around the room in a variety of armchairs, knitting or writing letters, peacefully. They looked surprisingly ordinary. Their blank faces glanced briefly at us as we passed, then returned to what they had been engaged in. I noticed how pale their ankles looked above their slippers. In the ward only four patients were propped on their pillows, and two nurses were busy making the other beds.

'This is Nurse Clouston,' Sister introduced me. 'Will you take care of her?' The 'phone was ringing and she darted back out of the ward.

'I'm Nurse O'Rourke. Have you done any nursing before?' one of the nurses asked me as I went round the other side of the bed to help her. My hands were trembling with eagerness as I tried to follow her quick movements.

'No, I haven't, I'm afraid.'

'You'll be in the school then?'

'No. I'm waiting till the new term starts.'

'Oh. You'll like it in the school though. We have a lot of fun, don't we, O'Brien? Here, let me show you how to do the corners.' She flicked the bedspread into place. 'That's all of those, thank heaven. Would you help me get Mrs Dean up now? She's just had an operation—a tumour.'

As we approached, an old faded face smiled up at us from under a crotcheted cap.

'How are you today, Mrs Dean?' Nurse O'Rourke shouted, then took a hearing aid from the locker and plugged it into the old woman's ear.

'Can you hear now?'

'Yes, yes, thank you,' she nodded eagerly.

'Wait while I get her chair.' Nurse O'Rourke moved off quickly, to return with a heavy wheelchair and a red blanket. While she had been gone, Mrs Dean had begun to slip slowly sideways on her pillow, still smiling foolishly. I had watched her, oddly fascinated, without making a move. Now I helped the nurse hoist her fat body off the bed.

'She can stand for a bit,' the nurse said, and added, raising her voice: 'You're standing well today, dear.'

'Yes, yes I am,' she smiled. But when we lowered her towards the chair she seemed to collapse into it and melt against the arms. Then her smile faded with childish suddenness. Her nightcap had fallen off and disclosed a shaven patch on her head. She glanced at us suspiciously as she clawed the cap out of her lap and fumbled it back on to her head. Then, miraculously, the smile returned. I wheeled her out into the sitting-room and was on my way back to the ward when Nurse O'Rourke called me into Sister's office.

'This is the Suicide List,' she told me in a conspiratorial whisper. 'Mrs Farrow's just gone on it. She was saving up her sleeping-tablets under her pillow. And Mrs Charles—she's the one in the red dressing-gown, that smokes so much. She used to be assistant matron—thinks she's getting her old job back, but of course, she isn't.' She ran quickly through the list. 'And that's why we must never leave the ward unattended. O'Brien's on now, but there must always be one of us. I've got a lecture at ten o'clock so I'll have to go soon. Have you had tea yet? You didn't come on till nine, did you? We usually have one about quarter past. You'd better have one now. Come and I'll show you.' She led the way out, glancing at her watch as she went. It was dark in the kitchen and two women were busy at the deep sink.

'Can we have this kettle, Maria?'

'Yes, luv. You're a bit late today, aren't you? There's wafers in the tin.'

Nurse O'Rourke pushed open the door of a little pantry and we seated ourselves among the shelves lined with biscuit tins and hung with blue cups.

'There should be some doughnuts around somewhere. I wonder who this belongs to?' She picked up a rock cake, sniffed it, then took a bite. 'What's in the tins?—empty, empty—ah. Iced wafer?'

'No, thanks. I think I'll just have this.' I sipped at my tea.

She shrugged. 'Wait till you've been here a while. You get that hungry on duty all morning. I'm on a long day today so I'll get lunch about quarter past twelve, but you'll have to wait till quarter to two. When's your long day?'

'How do you mean?' I looked blank.

'Didn't they tell you? One day, you work from quarter past seven in the morning till nine at night.'

'Oh, yes. Then you get the next day off?' I nodded.

'That's right. O'Brien and I can never get used to working on Sundays. Nobody works on a Sunday at home.' She rummaged in the tins again. 'I don't suppose you've tried the canteen yet?'

'No. Anyway, I'll probably go home.'

'Oh, you're living out then?'

'Yes, at Reigate. I'm flatting with a friend.' I thought cosily of Stephen.

'Oh, I don't think I'd like that. We have a lot of fun here—dancing and pictures, you know. And the canteen isn't bad. Thursdays, it's awful—and Fridays. They don't know how to cook fish. We have a lot of Irish nurses here, so we're mostly Catholics. And Jamaicans. What are you?—religion, I mean?'

'Oh—I was going to turn a Catholic once but I changed my mind.'

'Well, I think it's a lot of fuss, anyhow. We all get to Heaven in the end—that's what I think, anyway.'

'I thought Catholics believed no one but themselves went to Heaven?' I asked.

'Oh, I don't know all that.' She dismissed the subject with a last bite of her biscuit. 'Goodness. I must get to this lecture. I was late yesterday, too. No, you stay and finish. I'll tell O'Brien you're here. Rinse your cup out as you go.'

I returned almost immediately to the ward. Nurse O'Brien was studying a magazine at the bedside of one of the patients.

She was taller than O'Rourke and serious-faced. She signed to me and I went over.

'Are you any good at crosswords?'

'Reasonably,' I told her.

'Well, would you help Mrs Farrows with this? There are some new patients coming in and I've got to see to their cases.'

At one o'clock I was joined by a little Jamaican nurse with round, brown cheeks.

'I'm Nurse Pollock,' she told me briefly. 'You can go on to the lecture now.'

'But—I'm not doing lectures yet.' I looked bewildered.

'Oh, this is different. Every week Dr Bryant deals with one of the patient's case histories and we discuss it. It's quite interesting really.' She looked defiant, then added: 'In Doctor's room, next to Sister's.'

I went obediently in the direction she pointed. O'Rourke, O'Brien, the Sister and a large, forbidding staff nurse were already there when I arrived. I joined them in the seats along the wall, surreptitiously rolling down my sleeves as I saw they had done. Dr Bryant came in frowning, with one arm across his back and carrying a sheaf of papers.

'Well?' He crossed his legs and looked up with a smile. 'Who did you want to discuss today, Staff?'

'Mrs Baird, please.'

'Ah, yes, Mrs Baird. Very interesting case, that. What do you know about Mrs Baird?'

'She's an alcoholic,' Nurse O'Rourke volunteered.

'Yes, she drinks. Gin-and-tonic. A nice, clean drink—according to her. It might surprise you to know she was once a very gay person—very "Hail fellow, well met". But have you ever noticed how calmly she can talk about gruesome subjects—for instance, her brother's death (he died quite recently in a car crash) and remain quite impassive? It's almost as if part of her were dead. I suppose it is in a way. It was during one of her drinking bouts that she fell and damaged her brain. I'm afraid we can never bring it to life again, completely. Tell me, do you think Mrs Baird will ever be discharged from here?' He was looking at me.

'No,' I stuttered.

'Yes,' he contradicted me. 'She'll be discharged. But before long, she'll be back. All we can do is keep her health in reasonably good condition—but she'll go on deteriorating. I'm afraid she'll never be really well.'

I thought of Mrs Baird's sagging face with pouches under the eyes, and remembered how her discoloured jowls had wobbled as I hoisted her yellow limbs on to the bed-pan. Supposing I was ever to become like that? Where would I get any sympathy? I would merely repel people. I shuddered—then laughed at myself. After all, it was unlikely that I could turn into something like that overnight. But was there any disease which produced those effects more rapidly? I grew serious again. There was so much I didn't know about this world. But now the doctor was getting up to go.

'I'm afraid I'll have to leave early today,' he said. 'Could I see you for a moment, Sister?'

'We're off now,' Nurse O'Brien said in my ear. 'Are you coming to the canteen? You should see the way they cook things. The ovens—absolutely huge.'

'No, I think I'll go home. I want to do some shopping.'

'You'll have to walk down. There isn't a coach until the nine o'clock one. But come along and see the holiday lists with me before you go. I think they've changed my long day.'

I found my way with difficulty through the maze of corridors, back to the sewing-room to pick up my uniform. Running down the steps with the brown-paper parcel bouncing against my knees, I felt strangely exhilarated. I could hardly wait to get home and tell Stephen about the morning. Thinking of what his expression would be when he saw me in my uniform with the short, thick coat, I almost laughed out loud. Of course he wouldn't be home for a couple of hours yet. Remembering this I slowed down but caught sight of the bus at the end of the little lane, so I sprinted across the bridge to jump on to the platform. Extending my fare, I gulped to recover my breath and the cold air tasted like a drink of water. How hungry I was!

But as soon as the door of our room closed behind me, I began to remember the awful parts—Mrs Dean's fixed smile as she slipped sideways on the pillow—Mrs Baird, the alcoholic. I shook off my coat quickly and began to prepare myself some lunch. I had turned on the radio but it always took some time to warm up. It suddenly blared and I started, breaking the egg I was sliding into the frying-pan. Dripping egg white, I ran across the room to turn down the volume.

I was peeling potatoes for dinner when Stephen appeared in the doorway.

'Well!' He looked me up and down, then came over and kissed me. 'Hmm, they put enough starch in these things, don't they?'

'You're telling me. This uniform's standing out about an inch from my body. Wait till you see me in my cap, though.'

'It sounds as if it's been fun.'

'Oh, yes.' I sobered suddenly.

'Well, go on, tell me about it. I know I've got a morbid mind, but what were the patients like?'

'They seemed quite ordinary, really.'

'Disappointing,' he grinned.

'I'm on the curable ward. They put you there first.'

He nodded. 'Do you give them that shock treatment, or what?'

'Yes. And insulin. But no one had any today. It was quite dull, really.' I suddenly found I couldn't talk about it. 'Do you like corned beef? I've made a casserole.'

15

I WAS very tired during the next few days. My body had grown used to doing so little work during my two months' holiday. Now, the six o'clock rising, and the long hours spent on my feet, had taken it by surprise. As soon as I arrived home a sort of lassitude would overcome me. At the same time I was nervy and irritable.

'You're driving me mad!' Stephen exploded at me, one evening.

I looked at him without much surprise. 'Why, this time?'

'I don't know. You sit there and you sit there and you keep on sitting. All the time I'm willing you to say something or do something—but you just sit there. You don't notice anything.'

'I'm sorry. I'm tired.'

'I know you are,' grudgingly. 'But I can't understand—— How can you be happy just not doing anything? Don't you want to—live—experience things? Haven't you got some aim in life—something you want badly? I feel as if you're quite content doing the same things over and over. Doesn't the thought of it make you depressed? You're in a dead end and you seem to like it.' He glared at me defiantly.

'Well, I've got a new job—a career really. And I've only recently got you.'

'Yes, but—— Oh, there's something missing somewhere. You know what I am? Lonely!' He flung it at me. 'You make me lonely.'

'Why? I'm not stopping you from seeing your friends. Or am I?' I asked him.

'No. My friends are broad-minded. It isn't that. I just feel lonely when I'm with you. When I should feel completed and—fulfilled.' His voice rose with emotion, and he coughed with irritation at himself. 'If you'd just talk,' he went on more slowly, 'instead of sitting there, so drearily.'

'Well, why don't you start a conversation if it worries you?'

'I don't know. After a while I get beyond it—sort of hypnotized by your silence. It's awful. It has to be you that starts talking. Don't look at me like that. What is it? You think I'm theatrical, don't you? I can tell.'

This was exactly what I was thinking, and I tried hurriedly to summon up a reply. Instead I said: 'You don't seem to like me very much.'

'Maybe I don't like you much, tonight. But I still love you—unfortunately. I never wanted to. I didn't know how right I was. I love you and I'm lonely. And I can't buy any cigarettes.'

'Why not?' I was bewildered.

'I can't afford it,' he told me grudgingly.

'Well, is that my fault? I'm getting my wages and paying my share of the rent and stuff.'

'I didn't have to pay rent at home,' he reminded me. 'Not to mention extra for bus fares.'

'All right. Go home.' I felt my body stiffen.

'Don't be silly, Di. Come here. You know what's really the matter?' He was smiling now. 'I just realized it in school the other day. It's been getting me down.'

'What?'

'I love you so much. I keep on telling you. And you've never told me—if you do.' His voice had become jerky and urgent.

'Haven't I?' I tried to sound surprised.

'No. Never, never, never.' His tone suddenly hardened and he seemed to tense himself. I knew he was waiting for my reply and I made a desperate effort.

'Stephen. I do. I'm almost sure. I'm just scared to say it. Because I was wrong once.' It sounded trite to me, but Stephen relaxed against me and claimed my mouth in a grateful kiss.

'Darling, you're so sweet. Are you too tired to come to bed?'

· · · · ·

I had been working at the hospital for about ten days, when I found myself suddenly transferred to another ward.

'It's only temporary,' Sister told me. 'The regular nurses are off ill. Nurse Brooks will take you.'

Ward Eleven was an old ladies' ward. It smelt. It smelt of warm, sour urine, and dysentery and perspiration. The old women were clad clumsily in patched flannel dresses, wrinkled stockings and flowered pinafores. Some of them were in wheelchairs, misshapen or legless. The others just sat around, muttering and singing.

'I love London town,' an old woman was croaking, rocking her stool backwards and forwards.

'Shut up, shut up!' shouted an ugly woman with one long tooth. 'You b——, you filthy b—— b——.'

I turned to Nurse Brooks, but she was hurrying over to the other side of the room.

'Now, Martha,' she said coaxingly. The woman had a pair of thick brown bloomers pulled over her head. 'She's always doing that,' she explained, tugging them off. 'You can do without now, you silly girl. They're wet, anyway.'

I noticed pools of urine under several of the old women's chairs.

'Yes, I'd better clean those up,' Nurse Brooks nodded. 'If you'd be sewing buttons on that pile of frocks over there. It doesn't matter about the colours.'

I went and sat at the bench where several old women were playing with the buttons.

'Nurse, nurse. I want to tell you about our Charlie,' a woman called out to me, coming across the room.

'Her Charlie!' the long-toothed woman said contemptuously.

'Yes, our Charlie. He'll be home soon. What's the time?' She tripped and fell, bumping her head. I lifted her, repelled by the feel of her body under the warm flannel dress. That this should be a living person, living flesh, on a mind that was quickly dying, filled me with horror. She sat beside me as I picked up a frock and began to sew. Her hand was raised to her head in a puzzled way, but she went on earnestly.

'Our Charlie's coming home. You remember him? He helped you in with the cuckoo clock. Well, what's the time, what's the time?'

A grey hand clawed at me and I looked down to see a tiny, thin woman with a childish face and white hair. She was running her hands through this hair, showing a bony pink scalp.

'There's glass in it,' she told me nervously, and stuttered for a few seconds before going on. 'It's all in my hair. Where are the scissors, Nurse? I'll have to cut it. Where are they?'

'There are no scissors,' I said firmly, feeling the handle of those in my back pocket as I sat against them. 'And there's no glass either, dear.'

She muttered to herself for a few minutes and I caught the word 'Lavatory'.

'Do you want to go to the lavatory? Come on then.'

This ward was laid out in almost exactly the same way as Ward One, so I found the toilet with no trouble.

'There.' I arranged her on the seat and stood with the half door open, waiting. She had had no underclothes on, whatsoever. Her stockings were round her stick-like ankles. Her body had been light as matchwood. She went on muttering at a fearful speed as I shepherded her back to the sitting-room. Her milky eyes were imploring, and her thin hands flickered in and out of her hair.

'There's glass in it, Nurse. You see? You see? It was the party—all in the marquee—and my sister—my sister was lying down upstairs—had to see—and then there was glass in my hair—glass in my sister's hair—older than me—Nellie isn't coming here, is she? Want to go to the lavatory.'

'Come on, dear. You've been to the lavatory.' I sat her at the table and she went on talking to her neighbour. Nurse Brooks was attending to the woman who had bumped her head.

'She's fallen down again and she's bleeding now. She's a

cheerful old thing, but she won't sit still. There. No, stay there.' She turned to me. 'We'll have to get the tables out for their tea now. Could you be buttering bread? It's sliced in the kitchen. I've got the kettles on.'

I went into the dark room and began buttering the thick bread in desperate haste, listening to Nurse Brooks clattering the chairs and tables beyond the open hatch. My hands were shaking as I piled the slices on to the plates and tipped jam into the dishes.

'There's cake, too,' Nurse Brooks called. 'Don't put it all out—about half.'

I found the crumbly yellow cake in the cupboard and added it to the trays. The women were chattering excitedly, making their clumsy way to the tables. I moved round quickly with the heavy teapot as they called out impatiently.

'Nurse, I haven't had any bread yet.' A short woman, thick as a tree-trunk, and with a smooth, high forehead, turned worried eyes on me.

'Well, there you are then.' I spread her some jam hurriedly and moved on. The others were helping themselves greedily, then dropping what they were eating, absent-mindedly, on the floor, like children.

'Nurse, I haven't had *anything*.' An earnest voice pulled me round. It was the same woman, with the high forehead, and her eyes looked at me, hurt and reproachful.

'Yes, you threw it on the floor,' I told her, and tipped another slice on to her plate.

'No, I didn't, Nurse. I haven't had *anything*. I was feeding the baby. I'm married you see. I'm married, aren't I?' She showed me a piece of blue wool tied round her finger.

'Yes, dear,' I soothed. 'Well, eat your bread now.'

A staff nurse arrived soon after this and helped us clear away the mess.

'You two go to tea now,' she told us. 'It's quarter past four.'

'Better wash your hands in Dettol.' Nurse Brooks led me out to the cloakroom. 'We've got dysentery here. That's why the regular nurses are off. How do you like it? Bit different from One, isn't it?'

'It certainly is.'

'I used to be on here, last year. I'm on Five now. That's not so bad. This is one of the worst ones.'

The more normal atmosphere of the canteen was a relief. It smelt of warm bread and buttered crumpets. Nurse Brooks piled her tray high with brown bread and crumpets, and two little dishes of jam.

'You're not eating much.' She looked at me. 'You've got to go till nine.'

'Yes. I'm not very hungry.' I was feeling a bit sick.

'I've got a lecture after this,' she told me, eating quickly. 'Staff'll stay on with you till half past five. I'll be back by then.'

I managed to find my way back to the ward without much trouble. A pair of worried eyes were staring at me through the glass. The old woman watched anxiously as I unlocked the heavy door and re-locked it behind me. I found my hands fumbling as I did so, and they shook as I slid the big key into my back pocket.

'Come on,' I coaxed her. 'You don't want to go out there. It's cold out there.' It was all I could think of to say. She stared blankly and didn't move, so I began to walk on down the passage. An excited muttering made me turn round again. She had the door open! I dived back and closed it.

I hadn't locked it properly. I was flushed and my heart was beating disturbingly.

'You don't want to go out there,' I repeated, taking her flabby hand. 'What's out there?'

'Everything!' She looked back and whimpered.

We began to put them to bed at half past seven.

'It takes ages,' Nurse Brooks told me, pulling a face. 'Look, run and take the temperatures, etcetera, of the old dears in bed, while I get the commodes ready. You might have to fight with that end one.'

She wasn't the only one I had to fight with. We wheeled in the crippled ones first, and sat them on the commode while we tugged their stale-smelling clothes over their heads. I tried not to look at the short stumps of the crooked little woman I was undressing, but she shrieked at me:

'They got my legs! Look, they got my legs! I'll get all their b—— legs! Won't I! B—— legs!'

At the same time one of the women who had been in bed, got up and began charging round the room with her head down, butting the air.

'Goo, g'goo! G'goo!' She screeched.

'That's Fanny,' Nurse Brooks told me calmly. 'We'll get her back in bed later. She goes on like that all the time. She's quite young, too. She was in Ward One at one stage, having Electric Treatment. Makes you wonder, doesn't it? That's right, tie their clothes up in their stockings, if they haven't messed them.'

We had wheeled the commodes down to those patients confined to bed with dysentery, and were changing the filthy sheets, when one of the women, with a pointed, impish face, started talking to us.

'Have you got a boy, Nurse? Have you?' she asked us. 'Are you married? The night we got married now—ooh, that was something! He wouldn't put the light out, my husband, and there it was—big as that! I didn't half get a shock. And he was so impatient! "That's all you're getting for tonight, my girl," he said, "cos you're too small." '

Nurse Brooks laughed heartily. 'She's a sexy old piece, isn't she? See her eyes sparkle.'

The woman looked delighted. 'Yes, that's what he said. "You're too small." Ooh, I was too. T'wasn't half messy. Ooh, it is awful! Don't you get married, Nurse.'

'Help, better get this away! The almoner'll be round.' Nurse Brooks began to trundle the commode up the ward while I folded the screen up. I tried to stop my hands shaking as I dipped them in the Dettol bucket, but it only made my muscles ache, so I gave up and dried my hands jerkily.

'I wouldn't like to be on night duty here,' I said to Nurse Brooks, as we waited for the clock to move round.

'Why not?' she asked. 'There's nothing much to do, and there's a fire. They don't go having fits and things, like Ward Five.'

Stephen looked at me in amazement as I came in the door of our room.

'What's the matter?'

'Nothing. I was on a different ward.'

'You look funny.' He put his arms round me. 'What are you so cold for? Darling, was it awful?'

'Oh, darling——' I began, then looked away confused.

Stephen grinned at me triumphantly. 'Well, go on. I don't expect you will.'

'Yes, I will. Oh, Stephen, I want to tell you about it. Let's sit down and I'll tell you about it.'

'Aren't you hungry?'

'No. No, I feel so sick.' My voice spilled out of me, and I went on and on, talking about the grotesque old women, while Stephen listened silently, watching me curiously.

'I hadn't locked it properly. And I said: "You don't want to go out. What's out there?" and she said: "Everything."' My voice grew shakier as I spoke and I kept feeling an urge to laugh hysterically.

'For God's sake, you have changed.'

I noticed I was chewing the polish on my finger-nail, and thrust it away from me impatiently.

'Darling.' He stroked my hair. For once he seemed at a loss for something to say.

'Oh, darling,' I said for the second time. 'I'm so frightened.'

'What of?'

'Just of being alive! Do I have to go back to that place? You do think it's awful, don't you—all that stuff I told you?'

'It sounds just horrible.'

'Well, thank God for that.' I relaxed suddenly and before long fell asleep.

16

WITHIN a few days I was back on Ward One. After the old ladies' ward it seemed dazzlingly clean and efficiently run. There were several new patients, all of them bedridden, some with varicose veins, one with an injured back, which meant more bed-pans and more work generally. I was finding it harder and harder to get up in the mornings. Stephen would lie in bed, watching me with half an eye, while I fastened my apron with frantic fingers. Soon after this, I missed the morning bus and the coach which connected with it. I was in the cloakroom pinning my cap, when Sister came by and looked in.

'Oh, so there you are.' She watched me sarcastically. With the others she got on well, chaffing and teasing them in a friendly way, but my quietness and anxiety to please prompted her to be scornful and irritable with me. If I tried to make a joke of something, she would raise her eyebrows in silent surprise, then look as if she hadn't heard. I listened to her lecture in silence, then raised my eyes to meet her gaze.

'Well, you'd better get on and help Staff. It's ECT today. I don't know why you have to live out, anyway,' she added, as if to herself.

'Yes, Sister.' I hurried to the ward and grasped a heavy floor-polisher.

'We've done that, Nurse Clouston,' the staff nurse called out. 'You could sweep the verandah. And see how Miss Deer is while you're there. She's had insulin.'

The sun was shining timidly in the chilly glass verandah and specks of dust shone, suspended in it. Miss Deer was lying with her arms flung out across the bed, shivering violently. A sickly smell of perspiration hung about her.

'Are you all right, Miss Deer?' I asked her, as I bent down to sweep under her bed.

'Yes, thank you, Nurse. I haven't had my glucose yet.'

'Oh, you'll get that about nine o'clock,' I told her.

'Thank you, Nurse.'

Suddenly the glass doors rattled and Nurse O'Brien appeared on the step.

'Doctor's here,' she called out. 'Could you get the stretcher ready while we do the beds?'

The beds in one half of the ward were pushed together so as to prevent the patients from falling on to the floor during the artificial fit which the electric treatment produced. Nurse O'Brien and I waited at the doctor's door. At length, it opened, and the familiar stertorous breathing reached us as a patient was wheeled out. Together we hoisted the woman on to the bed and I waited beside her until the jerking limbs began to relax. Then I drew the breathing apparatus from her mouth and covered her with the red blanket. She had bitten her lip and a little blood oozed down her chin to mingle with the froth.

'Not so many today,' Nurse O'Brien called as the beds began

to fill up. 'You can start getting the end ones up now. Damn, there's no name on this mug. Do you know who these teeth belong to?'

'I think they're Miss Charles',' I volunteered.

'Oh, yes, that's right. These'll be her slippers, too.'

I was helping one of the patients out to the sitting-room when she looked up at me.

'When am I going to have the shock treatment, Nurse?' She leaned shakily on my arm.

'You've had it, dear.'

'No, I haven't.' She looked bewildered.

'Yes, it's all over,' I smiled at her.

'But—I don't remember——'

'Of course you don't remember.' I lowered her into an armchair, and signed to one of the other patients to fetch her a cup of tea. Sister's quick footsteps sounded behind me.

'Hurry up with that, Nurse Clouston. I want you to screen Mrs. Laing and Miss Druid. Dr Rhodes is coming to examine them.'

'Who——' I began.

'The ones with cradles on their legs,' Sister added impatiently. 'And I want you to take Mrs Moodie to the dentist, and drop this file into the main office as you come back.'

I was returning past the sterilizing-room when Sister darted out and grasped my arm.

'Nurse Clouston, I want you to wash down the lockers. Take them out to the cloakroom to do them. Not the ones of the patients in bed, of course.'

Nurse O'Brien was passing and raised her eyebrows at me over Sister's shoulder.

I had lugged the last of the heavy lockers back to the ward, and was busy washing down the bed of a patient who had moved to another ward, when Nurse O'Brien came over clasping a stone hot-water bottle.

'Sister's got a down on you today,' she said. 'You haven't had any tea yet, have you?'

'No.' I felt suddenly sorry for myself.

'Look, take this out to the kitchen as if you're going to fill it, and get yourself a cup. I'll do this.' She held out the hot-water bottle. But at that moment Sister's voice was raised in the sterilizing-room.

'Nurse Clouston! Come here!'

Trembling like a schoolgirl, I hurried to her.

'Is this your Dettol water? Then what's it doing here, for goodness' sake? Who do you expect to clear it away if you don't? You'll have to pull your socks up, my girl. And while we're on the subject,' she added. 'Haven't you got any better stockings than those? You're earning enough here to afford a pair of black stockings once in a while.'

I felt my mouth tugging at the corners in an urgent desire to cry. I was afraid to open it. Instead I looked at my feet. The stockings had laddered at the toe and the ladders had crept up over my feet. My suède shoes were covered with dust collected while I swept out the verandah. The sight disgusted me, but, at the same time, I felt unjustly insulted.

'Yes, and you'll have to get some other shoes,' Sister went on. 'Or at least some rubber soles. Those are disturbing the patients.'

I returned to the ward and silently continued scrubbing down the bed. Nurse O'Brien started on the other side with a second cloth.

'You're on a long day, aren't you?' she asked, after some time. I nodded. 'Well, at least you'll get off at quarter past twelve for lunch. I've got to put up with her till two. She's terrible today.'

At twelve-fifteen I hurried towards the canteen, buttoning my cuffs with trembling fingers. My hands still shook as I bore my tray with stew and apple pie to an empty table. I had forgotten to collect a coffee spoon, so stirred in the sugar with my dessert spoon. The atmosphere of the canteen was beginning to give me a sense of temporary security. Was security always to be merely temporary for me? I thought of how I would tell Stephen of Sister's lecturing me and tears of self pity came to my eyes. The green sugar-dispenser wobbled and steadied as tears kept threatening. I began hurriedly to eat, and felt better with each warm, tasteless mouthful.

I was raising my cup to my lips when the assistant matron came in, and I held it there, watching her absently over the rim while she selected a table. Suddenly I noticed my teeth were rattling on the side of the cup. I lowered it quickly, staring at it in horror. It reminded me of a comedy situation in a film—the kind of thing that would happen in a comic strip. And yet this was no comedy. It was real, and this was me it was happening to—these were *my* teeth rattling on the cup. A sudden hysteria overtook me. I would have to laugh or cry. Then the clock on the wall luckily drew my attention. I couldn't afford to be late a second time! Discarding my apple pie I returned to the ward.

In the afternoon a different sister was on duty—a gentle, smiling creature—and I sighed with relief. It was visiting day, and instead of having to stand with our hands clasped behind our backs, Nurse O'Rourke and I were permitted to sit at a table at one end of the ward, making swabs. I was so relieved to be off my feet at last that I found myself slouching carelessly in the hard chair. I was curious to see what kind of visitors each patient had, so watched the coated figures, which seemed so out of place in the ward, with half my attention. Nurse O'Rourke was chattering on about her 'boy'.

'We're getting engaged tomorrow,' she told me with a sudden casualness. ' 'Cos that's my birthday. You wouldn't like to swap your day off, would you? It doesn't matter if you don't want to.'

'No, that's all right. When's yours?'

'Wednesday. Only another day away. And you'd be on afternoons tomorrow.'

'Oh, good. As long as I don't have to get up early.'

'Do you like afternoons best then?' She looked surprised. 'Gosh, I think they're boring. But thanks, anyway.'

It was after tea, when I was clearing the flowers from the ward, when Mrs Baird, the alcoholic, spoke to me in her dead pan voice.

'Hallo, Nurse Clouston. You were on this morning, weren't you?'

'Yes, I'm on a long day today.'

'Oh, I see. I've got a sweet for you, Nurse. Help yourself in that drawer.'

I was moving off with her vase of flowers when a choking sound pulled me round again. One of the woman's arms was flailing, uncontrolled, above her head, while her face was turning an odd grey colour. I ran hastily for Sister, and bumped into Dr Bryant leaving his room. He hurried ahead of me down the ward, adding over his shoulder as he saw Mrs Baird's face:

'Better fetch the oxygen.'

I trundled the clumsy apparatus across the floor with noisy speed, and stood aside, clasping my hands together to steady myself.

'I think she'll be all right now.' Dr Bryant straightened up at last. 'Where did Sister get to, anyway?'

'I don't know.'

'Well, when the other nurse comes back from her lecture one of you'd better get some oxygen. That thing was nearly empty.'

I straightened the screens around her bed, then stood by hesitantly, wondering whether to go on clearing the flowers. A sound of vomiting sent me running for a kidney bowl. As I took it away from under her flabby chin, Mrs Baird raised unseeing eyes to me. They watched me dazedly as I covered the bowl, then all at once seemed to click into focus, and she cried out:

'Something's happened! What is it, Nurse? What's happened?'

'You're all right now,' I tried to reassure her.

'Something must have gone wrong. What is it? I'm frightened.'

These last words suddenly made me aware that Mrs Baird was not merely another patient, to be panned and blanket-bathed at regular intervals. She was a person—like myself. And she was frightened. I tried to smile at her confidently. Then I let out my breath with shaky relief as I saw Sister approaching down the ward.

I missed the nine o'clock coach that evening and had to

walk down the eerily shadowed steps. The room was in darkness when I got home. I switched on the light and Stephen sat up in bed.

'Good heavens, it's only quarter to ten.' I looked at him in amazement.

'I was tired,' he told me. 'I never get to sleep again after you leave in the mornings.'

'You're lucky you can lie in at all.'

'Are you in a bad mood?'

'No.'

'Well, hurry up and come to bed if you're coming.'

'I'm going to have something to eat first.'

'I'll go to sleep,' he threatened.

'Go to sleep then. I'm hungry.'

'Oh, all right.' He turned away from me.

I opened the cupboard door angrily and cut myself a piece of cheese. It tasted stale so I threw the remainder into the rubbish-bin.

'What are you doing?' he asked, as I sat on the bed to roll my stockings off.

'I'm coming to bed.'

'Oh, all right then.'

I pulled the blankets up under my armpits and lay stiffly on my side of the bed. Gradually Stephen's breathing grew heavy and regular. I shuffled in the bed and sighed exaggeratedly but he didn't stir. Hot tears swelled under my wide-open lids. I muttered 'Oh' impatiently and he half sat up.

'What's the matter?'

'Nothing.'

'Then go to sleep. Aren't you tired?'

'Yes. Tireder than you!' I flung at him. He had turned back to the wall and before long was breathing heavily again. I sighed loudly, then climbed out of bed snatching the eiderdown, which I took with me to the sofa. Huddled in a ball, I began to cry, quietly at first, then more fiercely until I was gulping and almost choking. When I had managed to get my breath back I sat up suddenly and shouted at Stephen:

'Wake up!'

'I'm awake. What the hell's the matter with you?'

'Don't you know?'

'No, I don't. For God's sake come to bed and don't be so silly.'

'No. I hate you. I don't want to touch you!'

'What?' He bounced out of bed and came over.

'I don't want to touch you,' I repeated more quietly. 'I'll sleep here.'

'You're coming to bed,' he said through his teeth, and suddenly he had lifted and deposited me there. I tried to sit up but he was hitting me angrily so that I fell first to one side, then the other. Then he made love to me with a sudden unaccustomed violence.

'You hit me.' I was still crying. 'You kept on hitting me.'

'Of course I did. Are you all right now?' he added after a pause.

'Yes. It was just that you wouldn't talk—I wanted to talk.' I was exhausted.

'We'll talk tomorrow. Sleep now,' he told me. 'Go to sleep.'

And before long I was sleeping.

17

'My throat hurts, my back hurts, I can't help it, Evelyn. Sister gets mad at me, Evelyn. I can't help it, Evelyn, can I, Evelyn?' I wondered who Evelyn was or had been, as I jammed the tap into place and turned the water on. The childish voice continued, coming ludicrously from the sagging, middle-aged body.

'Shall I get in, now, Evelyn?'

'Yes, in you get.' I helped her over the side of the bath and her discoloured legs floated out like two bloated eels under the water.

'Shall I do your back?'

'Yes, please, luv. You're not mad at me, are you, Evelyn?'

'No, I'm not mad——'

'They junk you in and they junk you out. That's what they do, Evelyn. They junk you in—— It's different where I come from. Everything's nice; and not just sometimes. Where I come from—it's nice and quiet—they don't junk you out—get mad at you. Good plain living, Evelyn. There's no snow, the place I used to be. Did you ever think it could snow like that, Evelyn? All that funny snow—and such a bright colour.' I stared at her in growing horror. It seemed as if—why, she could have been talking about Micald! I steadied myself on the side of the bath.

'Where do you come from?' I said unsteadily.

'Yes, where I come from. Ooh yes, rub it there, it's itchy.'

'Come on out now.'

She looked up in surprise at my changed tone. 'They junk you in and they junk you out. My throat hurts.' I turned the pages of the bath-book hastily and put a wobbly red tick at the side of Mrs Moodie's name.

'Are you coming for tea?' Nurse O'Rourke caught sight of me as I locked the bathroom door. 'You're looking awfully pale. Is it your time of the month?'

I shook my head. 'No, but I could do with a cup of tea. Is O'Brien on?'

'Yes. She's got a long day today.'

As we sat among the blue cups and biscuit tins with our tea, I tensed myself and turned to Nurse O'Rourke.

'Where does Mrs Moodie come from, do you know?'

She shrugged. 'Somewhere up north I should think. With that accent. Why?'

'Oh, nothing in particular.'

'She's a queer old thing, isn't she? They can't do much for her. It's organic you see.' She looked knowing. 'Sometimes she's quite all right. Then suddenly she goes like this. Have you taken her over to EEG lately?'

'Yesterday.'

'She keeps going to sleep in the chair, doesn't she, and it upsets the wriggles? I used to take her. Doctor made me stand behind her and cough to keep her awake. Are you all right?'

'Of course I am.'

'You do look pale. Mustn't let this place get you down. It

used to worry me a bit at first—used to think I was going a bit peculiar myself. I'd get a kind of tight feeling in my head. You don't get a tight feeling in your head, do you?'

'No.'

'Well, I still get it sometimes if I'm terribly worried about something. Do you know how you see if you've got a brain tumour? Stretch out your hand and I'll show you. No, you haven't—it would have curled up.'

I was taking Mrs Farrows for a test under the electro-encephelograph when she turned round with an amused expression, and said:

'I can walk. Why do I always have to go in this thing?'

'One of the regulations.' I skirted a bump in the path, balancing a tray of blood samples in one hand.

'Well, it just seems silly that's all.' She paused, then added aggressively: 'This is a mental hospital, isn't it?'

'It's a hospital for nervous disorders,' I said soothingly.

'Hmm. I used to work in one of these places. Cleaning and so on. Never thought I'd land up here. Funny, isn't it, Nurse?'

I swallowed. 'Yes, it is funny.'

'Of course, I'll be out of here any day now I expect. I wonder what they'll find out today with that machine. It's like going to a hairdresser's, isn't it? All those clips in your head. I do miss my trip to the hairdresser. I expect I look a fright now, don't I?'

All the time my mind kept darting back to Mrs Moodie and remembering things she had said—'no snow where I come from—such a bright colour'. Perhaps I was mad after all. Perhaps there was no such place as Micald. It seemed so misty and unreal now. But I couldn't be mad—Stephen wouldn't love me if I was mad. I remembered visitors' day and young Mrs Laing's husband bending down to kiss her. How did he feel? A shudder ran through me. I wanted to find Mrs Moodie and question her, till I found out what she had meant. Perhaps there was a simple explanation. And yet I was afraid to approach her—just in case.

That afternoon, while I was waiting for Stephen to come home, I glanced through some papers he had brought back from school and came across a sheaf of poems. I took several minutes to realize he had written them himself. When I did, I flushed—I'm not sure why—with annoyance or embarrassment. I read them impatiently and flung them down. They were obscure, but in some parts almost beautiful. I couldn't associate them with Stephen at all. I picked them back up and flushed again. Why was I so angry? Because he had kept them a secret? Because they were unexpectedly good? Before he came home I had decided on the reason for my anger. It was because he hadn't expected me to understand them. He didn't think I had ever experienced those kind of emotions. Perhaps I hadn't. A huge envy overcame me—a longing to understand the emotions Stephen had tried to describe. I was beginning to understand. In a little time——

Stephen came through the door and threw his satchel on the table, wrinkling the tablecloth.

'Hallo, darling. Why aren't you always on mornings? So nice to come home to the little wife.' He teased me.

'Stephen.'

'What's wrong?'

'I'm in a bad mood.'

'Why, for heaven's sake?'

'What are these?'

'Oh,' he reached out his hand for the poems. 'Have you read them? You're nosy, aren't you?'

'I'm *not* nosy. I thought you said we weren't to have any secrets.'

'And you didn't agree,' he reminded me, smiling faintly as he turned the pages over.

'Well, I've changed my mind.'

'You've changed your mind about a lot of things lately.'

'Well?'

'Well, what about these poems, anyway?'

'When did you write them? After we came here?'

'Oh, yes.'

'You mean, while I was sitting down reading the paper, you were busy working these out in your head?'

'I suppose so. And in the bath. And in bed.'

'How awful.'

'What's awful?' He was grinning openly now.

'You could have told me.'

'I didn't know you wanted to know.'

'Of course I wanted to know.'

'Well, that's very gratifying. What did you think of them?'

'Not bad.' I turned away sulkily.

'This one's about you.'

'Yes, I thought it was. Hand me the egg-beater, please.'

'Don't you like what it says?'

'It isn't my idea of myself.'

'What do you think you're like?' He was laughing at me.

'Not as negative as all that. Anyway, if I'm so dull, why did you want to marry me?' I turned round suddenly.

'I didn't say you were dull. You didn't read it properly. It was your withdrawnness that I found so tantalizing.'

'I'm not so withdrawn now, am I?'

'No, you've changed.'

'So I don't tantalize you any more?'

'A man doesn't want to be tantalized all his life.' He paused. 'Well, get on with the omelette. I'm hungry, you know.'

'You don't want to marry me now, do you?'

'Yes. But you won't, will you?'

'You'd get such a shock if I said I would, wouldn't you?' I jumped back as the frying-pan spat at me.

'Well, will you?'

'No.'

'There you are then. Di?'

'What?'

'Why are you in such a bad mood lately?'

'You said you'd make me happy, didn't you?'

'What do you mean?' He looked suddenly crestfallen.

'Well, I'm not happy.' I dumped the omelette defiantly on his plate.

'What haven't I done?' He moved towards me in concern.

'Oh, nothing. It isn't you. It's me that's the trouble. I'm sorry.'

'I'm not very happy either, right now.'

'Do you think we ever will be?'

'Get on with your dinner.'

'I said, do you think we ever will be?' I persisted desperately.

'I think you should give up nursing.'

'Why?'

'You don't like it, do you?'

'Sort of. It's interesting.'

'Fascinating, you mean. I think you're getting more morbid than I am.'

'Oh, I'm not.' I was horrified. 'It's just—well, I'm just getting used to it. I can't stop now. I'll be starting the course next month.'

'Did you get any mail today?' He spoke through a mouthful of spinach.

'No. I would have told you. I should have got one from home though, shouldn't I?'

'You haven't told them you broke off your engagement, have you?'

'No. But Robert will have told them.'

'Won't he feel a fool?'

'I expect so. Yes, poor Robert. I'm a bitch, aren't I?'

'When are you going to cancel your passage?' Stephen asked, looking at me suddenly.

'Oh—do you think I should?' I hesitated.

'Well, if you want to risk losing your fare money.'

'Oh—I think I'll leave it a while. Just in case. I mean, in case you leave me or something,' I added hastily.

'Di. I promised. Don't you believe in promises?'

'Not much.'

'Well, at least you should believe in me. That's why you're not happy, I expect.'

'No, it's me. It's me I don't believe in.'

'You mean you've got an inferiority complex?' He looked at me with a faintly mocking smile.

'No, nothing like that. I just can't be sure what I'm going to do next.'

'God, you're a funny girl. Everybody's got *some* control over their own destiny.' He stared at me.

'I'm not sure that *I* have.'

'Oh, you're crazy.' He rumpled my hair.

'Don't do that.' I jumped up quickly for my comb. As I pulled it through the tangles I looked out of the window down to the street below. A black spaniel was crossing the road at a leisurely, old-aged pace, as if he were dragging his feet in galoshes. The rest of the street was dusky and empty, except for an old man clipping his high hedge with long shears. The exertion was evidently making him perspire, for he suddenly clutched his old beret from his head and threw it on the grass behind him. I turned back to Stephen, smiling against my will.

'I like it here. It's wonderful. I don't want to go—anywhere else.'

'Darling, Di. Just as long as you don't change your mind about that. I like it too. I'll never forget any of this—or you. But you'll be there to remind me, won't you?'

18

About this time I began acknowledging to myself that I loved him. Looking back it appears strange that I shouldn't have acknowledged it sooner. At this time also, I noticed a growing change in Stephen. He was less talkative. In fact I often felt frustrated by a kind of lassitude in him—an unwillingness to pursue a conversation I had begun. I had relied on him to take the initiative formerly, to lead me on until he had extracted from me what he wanted to know, and what I was now secretly anxious to convey. Now I found it harder and harder to get him to talk.

'What's the matter with you?' I asked him one day.

'I don't know.'

'Then you admit there's something the matter?'

'Why did you ask me, anyway?'

'You just seem—subdued. Why don't you ask some of your old gang around sometime?'

'You sound like the typical wife,' he laughed at me, and added: 'I see them around.'

'Don't you miss your old life?'

'It hasn't changed much.'

'Oh, it must have.'

'Yes, I expect so. But I'm really quite happy, this way. The gang seem a bit childish now.'

'Oh? I wouldn't know.' He was silent, so I went on. 'You don't smoke your pipe any more. Or those long cigarettes.'

'What's wrong with these?'

'I thought you said they were dull.'

'Oh, yes. But you can't really beat them.'

'We haven't eaten out for ages. Remember that restaurant in Soho?' I looked at him earnestly.

'Remember the price,' he said briefly.

'All right, put your slippers on and get your feet up in your favourite armchair,' I chided him.

'Don't be silly. I'm not like that.' He looked suddenly annoyed, but didn't pursue the subject so I let it drop.

'How was school today?' I used to ask him regularly as we sat down to our evening meal.

'Oh, all right,' he would reply. One day he added: 'There's a new girl teaching the infants.'

'Oh, what's she like?' I pounced.

'Just a girl.'

'Pretty?'

'Sort of.'

'How do you mean—sort of? What's wrong with her?'

'Nothing's wrong with her.' He looked impatient.

'You mean she's perfectly proportioned, perfect features, perfect hair?' I looked at him in exasperation.

'I expect so.'

'Oh!'

He looked at me in surprise.

'Well, you could have at least found one thing wrong with her, so I wouldn't be jealous.'

'Oh, are you jealous?' He looked up in interest.

'Yes, I am now.'

'Well, all I'm saying is, I didn't *notice* anything wrong with her,' he told me.

'Was her hair nice?'

'Yes. Fair.'

'Fat?'

'No. I told you, no.'

'Well, you could at least pretend.' I was nearly in tears.

'Di, don't be silly. What would be the use?'

'Oh, go away. No, I'll do these myself. Read your silly paper—cover to cover.' I clattered the dishes angrily in the tiny sink. 'You could do all sorts of things while I'm on late shift,' I added after a few minutes.

'Well, I don't do I?'

'I don't know.'

'I'm telling you I don't. You said you were going to do the dishes, so do them.' He flipped the newspaper open.

'I'm doing them. I can talk at the same time. I don't suppose you can?' He didn't reply, so swirled the mop round the plates with careless speed while I felt my eyes growing hot. When I had stacked the dishes in the cupboard, I went impulsively and sat on the arm of Stephen's chair.

'Please, Stephen. Talk to me for just a minute. I'm so lonely.'

He smiled and pulled me down on to his knee. 'What's the matter, anyway?'

'You do love me, don't you?'

'Of course I do.'

'When did you start loving me?'

'Oh, ages ago.'

'But when?' I pursued.

'I don't remember the exact day. But I love you now, and that's the main thing.'

'Yes, I suppose so. What do you love about me, though?'

'Why, everything.'

'But there must be something specially——' I pleaded.

'There isn't, though. I love all of you.'

'Can't you think of something? You never pay me compliments.'

'If I do, you just tell me not to be silly.'

'Well, I won't this time.'

'I can't just pay compliments to order.' He looked down at his hands.

'No.' I gave a deep, exaggerated sigh.

'Oh, Di. I do love you. Do stop being silly. You're always analysing things these days. You can't analyse love.'

'You can, though. I think you just love me physically, anyway.'

'I don't, Di. There's more to it than that. They all get around to accusing you of that,' he added, as if to himself.

'Who's they?'

'Women.'

'Which ones?'

'Oh, I've told you about them.'

'Well, tell me again,' I demanded.

'No, I won't. Now shut up. I want to read this article.'

The following day was my day off, and I arranged to meet Stephen for lunch in Redhill. Waiting outside the milk-bar, pleased with the reflection of myself in a summer frock instead of the striped nurse's uniform, I saw Stephen reflected in the window. He was nodding good-bye to a girl in a red dress, before crossing the road to where I stood. I watched him come up behind me without turning round.

'What are you staring at?' He tapped me on the shoulder.

'Pleased to see me?' I turned to him defiantly.

'Yes. You're looking very nice.'

'Not as nice as Miss Whatsername, I suppose.'

'Miss who?'

'That girl—in the red dress.'

'Oh, so that's it. We just caught the same bus.'

'She's pretty,' I accused him.

'Well, I said she was, didn't I? Luncheon meat and chips?'

'Oh, I suppose so.'

'Well, you don't *have* to have them.'

'No, I won't. I'll have a mixed grill and eggs extra. Stephen, can you lend me some money? I've got five pounds at home to pay you back.'

'Of course. What did you want it for?'

'I'm meeting Kathleen and we're going shopping together. I need another frock. This is my only respectable one.'

'But you wear your uniform most of the time.'

'I suppose you're sick of the sight of me in it?'

'I didn't say that.'

'Well, if I got more frocks I'd change when I got home—after morning shift,' I told him in the aggressive manner which was becoming a habit with me lately.

It was a relief to see Kathleen's cheeky pony-tail bobbing from side to side as she ran across the road, darting to avoid a bicycle.

'I hope you're in a mad, spending mood,' she greeted me. 'I just saw a smashing evening sweater in Dawsons. Looks just like Audrey Hepburn. Whoops! Let's go in here. I want to see what they've got in long playings. Has Stephen fixed your pick-up yet?'

'No. I don't think he's unpacked it.'

'What's wrong with him? He's got loads of records. I'll have worn them out if he doesn't take them. What shopping have you got to do this afternoon, anyway?'

'I want to buy a summer frock, first of all. Then I'll see what money I've got over.'

'Does it have to be red?' Kathleen asked, as I stood in my slip in the mirrored cubicle. 'I like this one in green best.'

'I still like the red.'

'Please yourself. Goodness, don't I look funny from behind? My pony, I mean. Do you think I should cut it off?'

'No, I like it. I think I'll take the red one, thank you.' I turned to the assistant.

'And very nice, too, dear.' She hurried away on her flat heels.

We bought a pork pie and a box of strawberries and Kathleen came with me back to Reigate.

'So this is it.' Kathleen looked inquisitively round the big room. 'It doesn't look much like Stephen.'

'What did you say?' Stephen pushed the door which she was about to close. 'Are *you* here?'

'Yes, I've come to dinner. I was just saying I wouldn't have known this room was yours.' She began to strip her coat off.

'Well, it's half Di's too.'

'Naturally. But what about your pictures and things. Aren't you going to put them up?'

'You mean the ones you did?' he teased her.

'No. You've got lots of others.'

'Oh, yes. Well, I meant to one day.'

162

'Shall I get Jim to bring them over for you one night?'

'Poor old Jim.'

'Oh, he won't mind. Put your frock on, Di, and we'll see what Stephen thinks of it.'

He looked at me doubtfully as I paraded in front of the old sideboard.

'Well? You don't like it, do you?'

'It's a bit bright.'

'Bright?' Kathleen looked shocked. 'Don't be awful Stephen. You like bright colours.'

'I've gone off red lately.'

'You can't "go off" red,' Kathleen looked angry. 'I like it, anyway. I wish I could afford some more frocks. I expect you're going to refuse the strawberries we've got for dessert?'

'No, I won't do that, I'm afraid,' he grinned.

'Thank goodness you're not married to him.' Kathleen glanced at him in sisterly contempt.

I was trying to remember what colour strawberries had been in Micald. We had certainly had them. I supposed they had been grey. It seemed difficult to imagine.

'Remember that painting I did all in different shades of red?' Kathleen asked, when we had divided the pork pie between us.

'Who did you give it to?'

'I don't think I gave it to anyone, did I?'

'Yes, you did. Wasn't it Linda?'

'Yes, that's right.' He looked puzzled, then said: 'Have you ever noticed how much red there is all around you? It's been getting on my nerves lately. I saw a woman in a sort of tomato-coloured coat today and it made me feel quite sick.'

'Oh, Stephen!' Kathleen laughed. 'I think you should have got the green one after all, Diana.'

'No, he can just get used to it.' I heard the tears in my voice and looked away in embarrassment. I had suddenly felt that Stephen was moving further and further away from me, and a wave of panic turned the pork pie dry in my mouth. Stephen didn't talk much for the rest of the evening. As she was leaving Kathleen said to me:

'Don't worry. He's just being awkward on purpose. He'll be all right tomorrow. And I'll get Jim to bring those paintings and records over. Brighten the place up a bit.'

19

Two evenings later Stephen urged me to bed at a relatively early hour. I was pleased and moved up to him with a feeling of grateful reunion. Almost immediately his enthusiasm seemed to wane. He lay very still beside me.

'What's the matter?' My voice sounded harsh coming out of the tenderness which had been swelling inside me. I said more quietly: 'Don't you want me now?'

'I can't.' He turned his head away.

'Do I repel you, or something?'

'Don't be silly. As if you could.'

'Don't I attract you any more?'

'Yes, you attract me. But I can't tonight, so do shut up.'

'Well, why did you pretend you wanted to? You started it.' I muttered after a few minutes.

'I told you—I did want to—very much. I don't know what happened, any more than you do.'

'What does it feel like, then?'

'I don't feel *anything*,' he almost shouted.

I was silent for some minutes, then murmured timidly: 'Don't you even want to make me happy?'

'Of course I want—stop talking about it.'

'All right. Just kiss me then.'

When his arms were about me I said suddenly in a choking voice: 'Stephen—pretend I'm somebody else—somebody exciting, somebody you shouldn't be making love to. A redhead—a lovely sleek redhead——' I went on murmuring in his ear. At the end of it I fell back exhausted.

'You see, it worked,' I breathed at him.

'How do you mean, it worked?' he sounded suspicious.

'You thinking of a redhead.'

'I wasn't thinking of a redhead. Don't be so fantastic.'

'Oh, you liar. You must have. It wouldn't work when it was only me. Perhaps you were thinking of Miss Whatsername.' I began to cry.

'Oh, for God's sake. It was your idea, the redhead, and I didn't think of anyone but you.'

'Stephen—tell me about this Linda girl. Was she very important? Was she nice to make love to? What sort of things did she say? Stephen, I'm asking——'

'I know, and I'm going to sleep.'

'Oh, you pig. I suppose you said the same things to her, didn't you? And to that fat one?'

'Plump,' he corrected.

'I'm hard and skinny, aren't I?'

'Slim,' he muttered briefly.

'Oh, can't you say more than one word at a time?'

'Look, what are you getting at? I love you. I've said so often enough.'

'Not so much lately.'

'It would be just like you to count,' he muttered.

'Silly. But I can't help noticing.'

'Well, I love you.'

'You don't.'

His hand slapped my face.

'Well, I don't think you do,' I persisted, cowering away.

'Well, that's your fault. I'm telling you. You've only got to believe it.'

'All right, I believe it.' I gave in with a sigh. 'I'm sorry.'

'About time, too.' He kissed me briskly and turned over to go to sleep. Before long I slept myself and had a very vivid dream. I dreamt I was walking in an empty aerodrome with someone several inches taller than myself. It was dark, with no moon, but the stars were very bright, like flecks of snow in the sky. We had our arms about each other and began to walk, trying to keep our eyes fixed on a certain star. It was surprisingly difficult to do and soon we were laughing and staggering about like drunken things. The empty aerodrome echoed about us, and a wind came up like a tidal wave knocking us into the long grass by a wire fence. We clutched each other breathlessly and he kissed me.

'Darling.'

'That's the first time I've enjoyed being kissed.'

'Darling.'

'No, we mustn't stay here.'

'Yes, we must. You're soft and warm, like a cat or a bee.' He nuzzled my hair.'

'A bee?'

'Yes. Because you sting too. Like Friday night.'

'I didn't know that stung you.'

'That's 'cos you didn't know I was in love with you.'

'What?'

'Well, you didn't know, did you? Oh, darling. Robert couldn't love you like this.'

'Who said he did?'

'Well, didn't he?'

I was silent.

'Anyway, I'll hang around, Di. I promise. So if you want me—don't forget.'

'Oh, dear, now I feel all awful. Why did you have to get serious?'

'There, you see. You're like a bee. A little bumble-bee.'

Bumble-bee—the words rose to a loud hum and woke me.

Stephen was removing the kettle from the stove.

'Oh, it's Saturday.' I sat up sleepily.

'Yes, and it's ten o'clock already. You'd better hurry if you want to go to the laundrette before you go to work.'

'Couldn't you have gone?'

'I'll go with you. I'm not going on my own.'

I munched my toast absently. I was remembering my dream and how real it had seemed. Surely there must be some foundation for it? Could the man have been someone in my past life? I remembered vividly his heavy eyebrows and, more vividly still, his hoarse, urgent voice. I waited for Stephen to ask me what I was thinking. He didn't, so I said:

'I had a queer dream last night.'

'Oh, yes?'

'Yes,' I said a little louder. 'About someone I used to know in New Zealand. I don't think I've told you about him.'

'Who?'

'Michael.' The name popped out and I applied it to the dark eyebrows triumphantly. It seemed to fit.

'Oh, no. You didn't tell me.'

'It was a queer dream.'

'Oh, yes?'

I looked at him impatiently. 'He was rather nice—Michael. He had a super voice. Have you ever noticed how important a person's voice is? I could never make love to anyone with a common voice. Could you?'

'I haven't tried.'

'What was Linda's voice like?'

'Do you want that other piece of toast?'

'*No*, thank you.' I paused angrily. 'It made me feel a bit homesick for New Zealand and everything. My dream.'

'Do you want to go back?'

'Do you want me to?'

'No, of course I don't. Anyway, I've cancelled your passage. I said I was your fiancé.'

'What? Good heavens!' I was vaguely pleased. 'And supposing I'd changed my mind? You took a risk. When did you do it?'

'About a month ago.'

'All that time? Then when you asked me about it, you'd already——?'

'They've paid the money back to the Wellington office.'

'Oh, yes, Daddy paid it. What a shame.'

'Except the twenty-five pounds deposit which you can call for any time you like.'

'Oh, Stephen, you do love me, don't you?' I looked at him expectantly. Perhaps now was the time for a big reunion. But Stephen only said:

'Of course I do. Look, it's half past ten. If we want to get to the laundrette . . .'

.   .   .   .   .

It was very quiet at the hospital that afternoon. The ward was empty except for two cases of varicose veins, and Mrs Baird with her jug of orange juice beside her. I stood hidden from them behind a half-folded screen at one end of the ward, looking out of a window into the quadrangle, and sucking a toffee. I was thinking again about Michael and could feel him taking shape in my memory. 'Soft, like a cat or a bee.' I gave a delighted shudder. I had been plumper then. Supposing I went back to New Zealand, would he be waiting for me, as he had promised in my dream? Probably not. Anyway, it was too late now. Stephen had cancelled my passage and they were so difficult to get at short notice. Besides, I didn't want to go back. I didn't want to leave Stephen. That was the last thing. I reproached myself in horror. All I wanted—I realized this suddenly—was to make Stephen jealous. If I could only arouse him to some kind of emotion, as long as it startled him from this lethargy—perhaps the spell would be broken and he would be cheerful and impulsive again. I would almost be pleased if he were unfaithful to me. At least it would arouse remorse. I shuddered. No, it was hardly worth it. But what could I do? It was getting worse all the time. I jumped as a high voice spoke behind me.

'I've been taking Mrs Dean for a walk, Nurse. In the grounds. Sister said I could.' A pair of delighted bird's eyes sparkled above the red dressing-gown. 'And look how my hair's growing.' She began to unwind a scarf from her head.

'Yes, I saw it yesterday,' I smiled encouragingly.

'When do you think I'll be going home, Nurse?' Her smile suddenly faded. 'Doctor keeps saying wait. We've got to be sure, he says. They've taken half my brain away already.

I can't concentrate on knitting patterns like I used to be able. I was ever so quick at them. And I want to see my Angela. Poor little girl—without her mummy.' Her voice quavered.

'I'm sure you'll be going home soon,' I said quickly. 'You're doing so well.'

'Do you think so? We only adopted her a year ago and now she hasn't got a mummy again.' Her face crumpled and ran with tears as she clutched on to my hand. Tears of sympathy came to my own eyes, but I forced them back, and reassured her unsteadily. I felt tired all at once. I was so unhappy myself, and here I was having so many other people's unhappiness thrust upon me. Was it the same for everyone in this world? Then how did they bear it? I withdrew my hand gently and listened to her thin sobs subsiding.

. . . . .

Stephen was marking spelling-books when I got home.

'I got fish and chips,' I told him, stepping into the room.

'Good, I only had an egg for tea.'

He seemed in a better mood, so I talked on about my day at the hospital and let him eat more than his share of the chips. It was only after we had gone to bed and were lying in the light from the street lamp that my doubts returned.

'Stephen.'

'Yes? I was just about asleep.'

'This Michael I was telling you about——'

'Mmmm?'

'Do you mind him being in love with me?'

'No. Why should I?'

'I wouldn't like anyone else to be in love with you.

'Why not? It would prove I was worth loving.' He sounded sleepy.

'I wouldn't like it all the same. It would mean she had part of you that I didn't have.'

'What?'

'Well—it's hard to explain. She'd have her love for you. She might love quite different things about you, that I hadn't noticed.'

'It's beyond me.'

'Well, I just thought you might mind—Michael, I mean.'

'No, I don't. Satisfied?' And he settled down to go to sleep.

20

EVERY day I grew more frightened. Stephen was indifferent and sulky. I found myself talking a lot, especially late at night, and I would ask Stephen questions at intervals to see whether he was listening. He was always able to make satisfactory replies, and yet I suspected him of not paying much attention to the things I was telling him. I was obsessed by the idea of his going away. He couldn't go away and leave me in this awful world! And yet, I didn't want to go back to Micald. Before long, this became an obsession with me, too. I terrified myself with the thought that one night I may go to sleep and wake up in Micald. I dreaded each night as it approached. Darkness was a good breeding ground for my dread, and the room in shadow would grow sinister as I watched it over the fold of the sheet. I told Stephen I had been having nightmares, but he refused to take me seriously.

One evening I was really afraid to go to sleep—so afraid, that I wouldn't go to bed. I was convinced that when I woke up it would be in a world without Stephen.

'Let's go to the pictures,' I urged him.

'But it's half past eight. Why didn't you think of it sooner?'

'It's supposed to be funny,' I persisted.

'Oh, I don't want to go out now.' He sounded martyred.
'Please, darling. I want to forget everything for a while.'
'Read a book or something,' he suggested.
'No. That doesn't work. Oh, all right, I'll go on my own.'
'No, you won't.'

We argued about it for half an hour, by which time it was too late to go, anyway. Saying I was going for a walk, I slammed the door and ran down the stairs to the street. The evening was cold on my bare arms and the darkness crept over me in chilling waves. I walked quickly on the even pavements, hearing my footsteps echo on the other side of the street. I didn't know where I was going—I didn't know Reigate very well. I half expected Stephen to follow me, but the street behind me was still empty when I turned the corner.

I had walked for some distance when I came to a church—a small building with the door opening on to the street. The heavy, round catch squeaked as I turned and pushed it away from me. Inside it was almost colder than the street outside. The shadowed pews filed away from me to a simple little altar. It seemed strangely naked. The whole place was bare in comparison to the church near Cadogan Square. Even the smell was absent—the funny, mysterious smell. But the atmosphere was there. I could hear it breathing about me like some big, invisible animal. As I stood there it seemed to grow louder, heavier, as if it were waiting to pounce. Goose pimples ran over my arms and I leapt for the door. I was running up the street, crying and coughing, and I could feel my face drawn up tight with terror.

Under a railway bridge I stopped, panting, and leant against the damp bricks. A train was passing noisily overhead, and by the time it had passed, I had stopped crying. I began to walk home.

I hurried, suddenly afraid that I was lost, but it seemed no time before I reached the familiar concrete gateposts. Stephen was asleep. I crossed to the table, rubbing my cold arms, and switched the table-lamp on. Still he didn't wake. He had been reading a mystery thriller, *The Golden Eye*, and it was lying under the lamp. I sat down and began to read where he had left the book open. It was a story of sordid, perverted crime, and I turned the pages in fascinated horror. I was still reading, the lamp growing pale against the daylight, when Stephen woke up.

'What the hell? Haven't you been to bed?'

'No. I was reading.'

'You've got to go on duty this afternoon.'

'I know.'

'You'd better get some sleep instead. Maureen'll ring up and say you're not well.'

'Oh, no. I'll go. I don't feel tired.'

We had a silent breakfast, and Stephen left to catch his bus. I lay for a moment on the unmade bed to finish my book. The rag-and-bone man was calling in the street below. A funny, eerie call, it sounded to me, in my sleepless state. I listened harder to make out his exact words.

It didn't seem long before I woke. I sat up smiling rather foolishly. My head was heavy, but at least I had had some sleep and was still in this large, untidy bed. I opened the cupboard door and lifted out the breadboard to make myself some lunch. I felt a sudden peculiar affection for all the now familiar objects in our large, shabby room. Then I noticed the time. It was after three o'clock—too late for me to go to the hospital. I remembered Stephen's suggestion and took some pennies down to the hall, to telephone. Maureen was quite concerned.

'Are you getting the 'flu or something?'

'No, I'm just worn out. I couldn't face going on duty today,' I told her. I could see the landlady listening at the end of the hall and turned to stare at her defiantly. She went away.

'Perhaps you'd better have tomorrow off, too,' Maureen suggested.

After a moment I agreed.

Stephen made me take two A.P. Codeines that night. I swallowed them with a strange feeling of fatalism. One half of me was convinced I had signed my death warrant in this world. The other half was relieved that the question of sleep was out of my hands.

I was still sleeping when Stephen left in the morning, and I woke to an empty room, buzzing with flies. I remember the flies particularly. They were all part of the horrible, brooding atmosphere. My mind had grown dark with apprehension, and I felt as if I was looking out on to the sunlight from somewhere deep and a long way off. I wandered about, touching objects in the room and handling them absently. My finger-tips seemed especially sensitive, and so did my tongue. I could feel it in my mouth, curled tight as if waiting for something.

Suddenly terror gripped me. I was aware of a feeling of compulsion. I was going to be forced to do something against my will! The feeling was so strong and stayed with me long enough for me to wonder about it. Fantastic ideas leaped into my brain. Was I going to jump out of the window? Throw the breadboard into the glass doors of the sideboard. I stood still in the middle of the room, looking round suspiciously.

Then I had my idea. There was a chemist's shop on the corner, at the end of the High Street. I chose a henna rinse carefully. The chemist glanced at my hair inquisitively and I stared back in irritable defiance as I handed across the money. I almost danced through the gateposts and up the dim stairway. With red hair—if it was as red as the girl's on the packet—I couldn't return to Micald. There I would be more than a freak. I would be an impossibility. There was just no such colour in the spectrum. I lit the geyser in the bathroom with trembling fingers. The darkness had gone out of mind and it was burning with a bright, white light. I turned the rinse into the cup and stirred it viciously with the end of the wooden spoon. The powder burst into startling colour, intoxicating in its very ugliness. Then a paler scum gathered on the surface, hiding it momentarily.

I sat by the window with my hair bound in one of Stephen's bright beach towels, and watched the street below. I looked contemptuously at the passers by—frowning or complacent, but always hurrying as if they were important enough to be needed anywhere. I laughed out loud and turned up the radio. The Critics shouted at me, then laughed drily and intellectually among themselves. I snapped off the switch and went to the mirror. There were fly spots on the glass and I removed them carefully with the edge of the lace duchess set before beginning to unravel my turban.

The hair fell out about me, damp and still streaked with uneven moisture—but red! A horrible, wonderful red! The room sang! And then I heard Stephen's voice in my head.

'I've gone off red—it's been getting on my nerves lately—it made me feel quite sick.'

My face tightened defiantly. I arranged myself on the sofa facing the door and waited for him to come home.